Handbook

for

Proofreading

Handbook
for
Proofreading

Laura Killen Anderson

NTC Business Books
NTC a division of *NTC Publishing Group* • Lincolnwood, Illinois USA

Library of Congress Cataloging-in-Publication Data

Anderson, Laura Killen, 1938-
   Handbook for proofreading / Laura Killen Anderson.

     p.   cm.
   ISBN 0-8442-3265-3 : $24.95 — ISBN 0-8442-3266-1 (pbk.) : $12.95
   1. Proofreading.   I. Title.
Z254.A5   1990
686.2'255—dc20   90-32808
                                                        CIP

1996 Printing

Published by NTC Business Books, a division of NTC Publishing Group,
4255 West Touhy Avenue, Lincolnwood (Chicago), Illinois 60646-1975 U.S.A.
Manufactured in the United States of America.

   6 7 8 9 VP 9 8 7 6

CONTENTS

INTRODUCTION

The written word is often the first impression a business makes on a prospective customer or client. If it isn't spelled right, if it isn't punctuated right, if it doesn't look good on paper, the business loses credibility.

Ideally, everything written in any office should be read for errors—typographical, spelling, grammatical, punctuation, and format—whether it is an annual report, an in-house publication, advertising copy, or a business letter. But even in those offices where the copy has been *read* for errors, mistakes slip through. More often than not, the reason why this happens is because the copy was not *proofread* by a person trained for the job. There is a difference.

Some people, even aspiring proofreaders, do not understand what the word *proofreader* actually means, how proofreading differs from any other method of reading, or what distinguishes the proofreader from any other kind of reader. Following are definitions of all three: the title, the job, and the proofreader.

The Title. Taken literally, the word *proofreader* is a present-day misnomer. The name dates from the advent of the printing press. "Proofs," or first runs of printed copy, were pulled from the press so that the "proof reader" could check them for typographical errors. When the typewriter was invented, another kind of "typo" wasn't far behind. Because the task of reading for typed errors remained virtually the same as reading for printed errors, the title *proofreader* stuck. So whether reading for errors on typed copy, from a desktop terminal, on a reader's proof, mechanical paste-up, or printer's proof, the one who performs the task is a proofreader.

The Job. In its most fundamental form, however, the job itself has changed. Computerized typing and typesetting, programmed with spelling and hyphenation checks, has encroached upon the proofreader's original domain, threatening to eliminate those readers whose talents are limited to catching the most obvious mistakes.

But for the reader whose knowledge and interest lie beyond the eternal typo, computerization provides both relief and challenge. What was once a restrictive, often tedious occupation is now an exciting opportunity to help ensure perfection through every step of the process and to become a far more valuable member of the communications team. For even the most sophisticated desktop equipment—now featuring grammar and punctuation checks, typesetting, and graphics capabilities—has not yet eliminated the need for a final, human stamp of approval. The system is still only as smart as those who operate it. And proofreaders who capitalize on both its advantages and failings not only increase their worth to the company but also widen their employment horizons immeasurably.

Technology has indisputably changed the proofreader's job requirements forever. As a result, employers are beginning to change their hiring standards. Proofreaders who can meet those expectations are being offered a higher salary and much more responsibility.

While proofreading is only one link in the "communications chain" (the progression of the written word from conception to production), the skills called upon are some of the most essential. The modern, state-of-the-art proofreader can save the company expense and embarrassment by catching a variety of obvious and not-so-obvious mistakes before they reach the costly stage of print—and the ever-critical eye of the intelligent reader.

The Proofreader.   Finding this kind of proofreader—or becoming one yourself—isn't easy. The job calls for technical knowledge of both language and print. It requires an aptitude, both inherent and acquired, for reading. And through each stage, it demands expertise and adaptability to the job at hand.

From typed concept to print, the copy passes through many stages and through numerous hands. And as it is evident in the stages outlined below, the proofreader plays a central and essential role in the entire procedure, reading the copy for the different kinds of errors that can occur at each stage of development.

This is what actually happens to the copy and the activities of those involved:

Stage One:

> ▶ Writer writes copy.

> ▶ Editor edits or revises copy.

> ▶ Typist types copy with editor's changes.

▶ Proofreader reads, queries, and corrects.

▶ Typist types corrections.

▶ Proofreader checks corrections, then reviews entire copy.

Stage Two:

▶ Artist writes type specifications on the copy and sends it (with layout) to typesetter.

▶ Typesetter sets type, makes reader's proof.

▶ Artist and proofreader read proof for errors.

▶ Typesetter makes corrections, sends back camera-ready proof.

▶ Proofreader and artist read corrections.

Stage Three:

▶ Artist's studio prepares mechanical art.

▶ Artist and proofreader read mechanical art.

▶ Studio makes changes or corrections.

▶ Editor, writer, artist, proofreader, and client (if there is one) read mechanical and approve (usually by signature or initial on the back of the mechanical board).

Stage Four:

▶ Production manager sends mechanical and artwork with instructions to printer.

▶ Printer makes negative and sends printer's proof to production manager.

▶ Final reading by production manager, artist, writer, editor, and proofreader.

Stage Five:

▶ Copy is printed.

Because the proofreader must lend support to the writer, the editor, the typist, the artist and studio, the typesetter, and the printer, you should have a basic understanding of what each is trying to accomplish and the skills involved. The more you know about their roles, the better proofreader you will be. The proofreader's tools (see Appendix A) will help you achieve that goal. And, step-by-step, this book will guide you through the process.

This book is not only for proofreaders, but also for editors, writers, desktop publishers, office managers—in fact everyone who strives for perfect copy.

For those who are not yet proofreaders, the book will explain the tasks and identify the skills that are needed to perform them. The chapters are mutually dependent, each one building upon the next. The beginner should read them in the order in which they are written. Study the book, use the tools recommended in the following pages, and practice your new skills at every opportunity.

For veterans of proofreading, this is an opportunity to enhance your skills, put more variety in your work, and get more satisfaction from it. The book may even reveal some secrets to proofreading you haven't already discovered.

1 | WHO PROOFREADS

THE WRITER AS PROOFREADER

Everyone is a proofreader, or at least most people go through the motions of proofreading every day. Whatever you have written or typed, there is a natural tendency to check for accuracy. Chances are slim, though, that you will catch all your mistakes, even if you read it a second time.

Why? Any experienced proofreader—or a writer who has learned from experience—will be quick to tell you: *Don't proofread your own copy!* It's difficult to look at your own creative work with a critical or unbiased eye. You will see only what you expect to see.

Many writers work without the benefit of staff support. They must write, type, and proofread their own copy. If you work alone, put some distance between the time you write and when you proofread, hours if not days. The longer you wait to re-read your copy, the greater your chances for a fresh, disinterested approach.

The real secret to proofreading your own copy is reading it slowly and critically, as though someone else had written it. It's hard to do, and that is why proofreaders are still in business.

THE ASSEMBLY-LINE PROOFREADER

In an office environment where there is no official proofreader, the job is most likely a shared one among those involved in a project—the writer, the editor, and the typist. It's logical that the more in-house exposure the copy gets, the more errors will likely be caught. So it should be read by as many people as possible, some who are familiar with the material and, most importantly, others who are not.

There are disadvantages to assembly-line proofreading. None of the readers may be trained to spot the many kinds of problems that can occur. Also the lines of responsibility may become vague, creating a situation where no one is truly accountable for uncorrected errors.

If your office uses such a system, do it with caution. Divide the proofreading duties outlined in these chapters among the readers, giving each a job in which they feel comfortable and have a certain degree of expertise. The best reader (most likely the editor, if there is one) should always be the last reader to look at the copy.

THE DESIGNATED READER

The ideal situation is to assign one qualified proofreader (or several if the volume of written material is high) whose only job is to find and correct errors. This is where the buck truly stops. The trained proofreader either catches all the mistakes or the blame for missing them.

Managers may be tempted to designate a proofreader from within their present ranks. That is a good idea, if there is one available with all the required skills. For the more familiar the proofreader already is with company policy and style, the more assured everyone will be of getting the job done quickly and correctly. If you are the one assigned this special duty, make sure this new task preempts other duties. Actually, other duties should be eliminated altogether, giving you the necessary time, solitude, and encouragement for thoughtful and accurate reading and inquiry.

If there is not one who is qualified or who is free from other office chores, the manager will probably consider hiring a proofreader from outside the company. While past experience, good recommendations, an understanding of type and design, and preferably a degree in English are solid prerequisites for the job, many employers may also test for specific skills and knowledge, incorporating problems that are peculiar to their business. This is an excellent way to judge firsthand the expertise of applicants. If you are applying for a job as proofreader, you shouldn't be surprised if the prospective employer demands proof that you are the right one for the job.

IDENTIFYING YOUR SKILLS

What qualifies you as a proofreader may vary from business to business. And the duties you will have as proofreader may be just as unpredictable.

As a writer who must proofread your own work, you will have not only the privilege of total authority, but also the burden of complete responsibility, so your proofreading skills must be exceptional.

If you are among the procession of assembly-line proof-readers within an office, you will correct as many errors as you know how to find and hope the other readers will catch what you missed. Or if duties have been divided among the readers, you will only be responsible for errors caught, and missed, in that particular area. Learn all you can about your assigned task. If you are not already an expert, work toward becoming one.

Skill requirements of the designated proofreader will be defined in your job description and will depend entirely upon the particular needs of the business. You should know those expectations before you accept the job and be prepared to meet them all.

LEVELS OF PROOFREADING

Beginner: Catches only deviations from the original copy, misspellings, incorrect math, incorrect word breaks, typing errors, format style.

Intermediate I: Duties of Beginner plus grammatical and punctuation errors.

Intermediate II: Duties of Beginner and Intermediate I plus typeface identification and type specifications.

Intermediate III: Duties of Beginner, Intermediate I, and Intermediate II plus advanced knowledge of language and type.

Senior: All of the above plus some copyediting skills.

MATCHING THE SKILLS TO THE JOB

The nature of a business signals implicit expectations about your skills. For example, in a publishing or editorial office, you will be expected to know (and care) more about word usage, grammar, and punctuation than in many other office environments. At a typesetting shop or printing company, you will often need more expertise in typeface identification, type specifications, and print production than you'd be expected to have elsewhere. And at an advertising agency, you will often need both skills in large quantities.

These businesses make the greatest demands on their proofreaders. Plus, working hours are often long and turnaround is short. If the businesses don't produce perfect copy every time, they're in trouble. So they must hire the best and most experienced proofreaders they can find.

There is also a broad range of other businesses with an equally diverse range of expectations. So it is important that you know what kind of proofreading you do best, and what level of proofreading you have reached or aspire to reach.

Get all the information about a prospective job before you accept it. You may be agreeing to more than you are qualified for or are interested in. Or you may become bored with the limitations imposed upon you. Find a situation in which you will be most happy in terms of interest, skill requirements, authority, challenge, advancement, and salary. An underqualified, overqualified, or discontented proofreader will not make a good proofreader.

2 | WAYS TO PROOFREAD

There are two ways to proofread, and how you do it is determined by what physical form the copy is in, as well as what stage of proofreading you have reached. Are you comparing one piece of typed or typeset copy against another? Are you proofreading from a computer screen or printout? Are you reading the copy for the first time, or are you re-reading it?

COMPARISON READING

When you must compare two pieces of copy to make sure they are identical in every way, you are comparison reading. During this reading, you will make sure that the newly typed (or typeset) copy is exactly the same as the original text, in terms of word sequence and format. You will also watch for misspellings, bad word breaks, and typing mistakes at this stage, but you won't use this reading to create your style sheet or look for any other errors or points of style. That is the purpose of subsequent, non-comparison readings.

There are several ways to comparison read:

Reading Alone

You will compare the original manuscript (dead copy) with the newly typed version (live copy), or if the copy has reached the typeset stage, compare the typed copy (dead copy) with the typeset copy (live copy). The newest version of the copy is always considered the live copy. The copy you compare it with is the dead copy. (See Table 2-1.)

TABLE 2-1. COMPARISON READING		
Dead Copy	**To Be Read Against**	**Live Copy**
Original Copy.		Typed Copy
Typed Copy		Typeset Reader's Proof
Typed Copy		Mechanical Art
Typed Copy		Printer's Proof

If you are right-handed, place the dead copy on your left, the live copy on your right. Left-handed proofreaders will place the dead copy on their right, the live copy on their left. In other words, the copy you will be correcting is always nearest the pen in your hand.

Place a short, nontransparent ruler under the line of the dead copy you are reading; place another ruler under the corresponding line in the live copy. This keeps your eyes focused on a single line of words instead of falling to the mass of lines below. It also keeps you from losing your place in case your reading is interrupted.

Now you are ready to begin. Read a few words from the dead copy, then read the corresponding words on the live copy. Continue reading from dead to live copy from beginning to end.

Reading with Another Person

This is a more efficient and interesting way to comparison read. The copyholder reads the dead copy aloud, word for word, including punctuation and format, while you proofread the live copy. Just as when you are comparison reading alone, you will read only for deviations from text and format, misspellings, typing errors, and incorrect word breaks. (For more details, see Reading with the Copyholder, page 11.)

Using a Tape Recorder

Whenever there is no copyholder and the copy is long or difficult to read, a tape recording of the original (dead) copy will make comparison reading easier for you. As you record, you should read the copy slowly, enunciating every syllable, every punctuation mark, capitalization, paragraph beginning, and format instruction. Then proofread the live copy as you listen to the recorded version.

NONCOMPARISON (OR DRY) READING

There are times when the proofreader will have only one set of copy, the live copy, to read. There will be no dead copy to compare your live copy with. Or you may have already compared the two and are ready to move on to the second stage of proofreading the job. You will be working alone at this stage, without the aid of dead copy, a copyholder, or a tape recorder. But you need not work quietly. Reading aloud, you will often hear mistakes that might have been missed during a silent reading. Hearing the words produces a sharper mental image of them and how they are used.

After Comparison Reading

After the newly typed (or typeset) copy has already been compared with the original text, your second, third, and any other passes will be those of noncomparison reading. From these dry readings, you will follow the proofreading checklist and create the style sheet. (See Proofreading Checklists on page 23, and The Style Sheet on page 26.)

On-Screen or on a Printout

Noncomparison reading is the only way to proofread when there is no dead copy to compare the live copy with, such as when you are proofreading from a computer screen or printout.

Desktop publishing equipment is becoming more widespread in the office environment and many employees, including the proofreader, have personal terminals. These terminals are often used as copy relay stations between writer and editor, editor and proofreader, and proofreader and typist. As the copy is passed to each in such a direct fashion, comparison reading is useless. The terminal screen *is* the copy. And a printed version (printout) is identical to what is on the screen.

It works like this: The writer composes the copy at a terminal, runs it through a programmed spelling and perhaps even a grammar check, then electronically transmits the copy to the editor's terminal. The editor has two choices in handling the material: (1) Editorial changes can be made on-screen, and the entire text is then transmitted to the proofreader's terminal for proofreading. (2) The editor can request a computer printout, which is a printed version of the on-screen text. This method is usually preferred by editors, as it provides a permanent record of the original copy and the editorial changes.

Access to a computer terminal gives the proofreader the same two choices. If copy is transmitted through the computer to the proofreader, corrections can be made at the terminal. However, some readers complain that on-screen proofreading creates problems in communicating with the writer or editor. When there are queries, the proofreader must list them in handwriting or type them on paper, identifying the precise on-screen location of the point at issue. The writer or editor must first refer to the written query, then go back to the terminal to make a decision. It could be a long, tedious process, and the old expression "it's all there in black and white" could be a welcomed convenience to the writer, the editor, and the proofreader of computer-originated text. If there are many queries or corrections, you may feel more comfortable reading a printout.

But for the high-tech proofreader, the disadvantages of on-screen proofreading can be outweighed by the speed and ease of correcting at the terminal. For example, one command will correct an error, another command will correct the same error throughout the copy—all without the bother of having to write it down. And queries may be so minimal that they create no real nuisance in communicating to the editor or writer. Because of this convenience, however, you may be tempted to "correct" something that, on a printout, you would have only questioned. Yielding to this temptation could cause trouble. What you suspect as an error could be intentional by the writer. Keep the editor or writer informed about all your corrections.

After the editing and proofreading have been done either on-screen or on a printout, and the corrections keyed into the computer terminal, a final hard copy should be printed out. This copy is then read by the writer, the editor, and the proofreader. (You will read by the noncomparison method if corrections were made on-screen, but read by the comparison method if corrections were marked on a printout, then keyed in.) Make sure all changes and corrections have been made. And watch for new errors entered accidentally while the old ones were being corrected.

BACK TO COMPARISON READING

This hard copy now becomes the dead copy and will accompany the job throughout production. The proofreader will use it for comparison reading, from beginning to end, at each stage, making sure that the hard copy is in complete agreement with the typeset proof, the mechanical, and finally the printer's proof. After the initial comparison reading with the hard copy at each stage, re-readings of the live copy will be noncomparison readings.

As the job progresses from the typed to typeset stage, the more expensive the errors will be to correct. So make sure you catch them as they occur in each stage.

READING WITH THE COPYHOLDER

The copyholder is a valuable commodity for a busy proofreader, especially when the text is long or handwritten, or if it contains many editorial changes or rows of numbers.

There are no extraordinary skills required for the job except an ability to read aloud. The copyholder can be anyone you are lucky enough to enlist, from the mail room clerk to the editor-in-chief. Most often, the copy typist is selected for this special duty.

The procedure is simple. While you concentrate all attention on the live copy, the copyholder reads the dead copy aloud to you, articulating every syllable, spelling words if necessary, noting punctuation marks, capitalization, and format instructions. This voice-and-scan process eliminates your having to juggle both the original text and the newly typed or typeset copy, an awkward procedure by which you could easily miss a deviation from the original text.

Voice Rhythm

The copyholder should read distinctly and as slowly as the proofreader thinks is necessary, repeating words, phrases, or entire sections if you need them re-read. The copyholder also should strive for a smooth, unbroken reading rhythm, avoiding unnecessary stops and starts or erratic pauses, and resisting interruptive and irrelevant comments about the copy. The only pause the copyholder should make is when you have stopped proofreading to make a correction.

Unfamiliar or Foreign Words

Although the copyholder may be tempted to pronounce an unfamiliar word or foreign words, what may seem the correct pronunciation to the copyholder may be quite different from the way the word should actually be pronounced. The copyholder should not hesitate when these words appear, or attempt to pronounce them, but instead spell them out letter by letter. In the case of foreign words, accent marks also should be indicated to the proofreader by the copyholder.

Copyholder's Vocabulary

Just as the proofreader uses a unique language to communicate (proofreader's marks), the copyholder also has a special way of communicating. It is an abbreviated way of reading numerals (to distinguish them from spelled-out numbers), punctuation marks, underscores, capital letters, copy layout, and typeface changes. Using the copyholder's vocabulary is, of course, optional, but the clarity and speed it provides is worth the effort to learn it. A little practice makes it easy. And it will soon become an indispensable tool for both the copyholder and the proofreader. The most common "words" are listed in Table 2-2 and Table 2-3. Following is a sample of copy as seen and heard by the proofreader.

The copy as it looks to the proofreader:

Whether you're still in school or you head up a corporation, the better command you have of words, the better chance you have of saying exactly what you mean, of understanding what others mean—and of getting what you want in the world.

English is the richest language—with the largest vocabulary on earth. Over 1,000,000 words!

You can express shades of meaning that aren't even *possible* in other languages. (For example, you can differentiate between "sky" and "heaven." The French, Italians and Spanish cannot.)[1]

The copy as it sounds to the proofreader:

whether you pos r e still in school or you head up a corporation com the better command you have of words com the better chance you have of saying exactly what you mean com of understanding what others mean em dash and of getting what you want in the world dot new pare english is

---

[1]Randall, Tony. "How to Improve Your Vocabulary," *Power of the Printed Word* series. New York: International Paper Company, 1982.

the richest language em dash with the largest vocabulary on earth dot over fig one com thou com thou words bang new pare ital you end ital can express shades of meaning that are n pos t even ital possible end ital in other languages dot pren for example com you can differentiate between quote sky unquote and quote heaven dot unquote the french one up com italians one up and spanish one up cannot dot close pren

It is not necessary for the copyholder to say "one up" for a capital letter at the beginning of a sentence. But if there is the likelihood of the proofreader misunderstanding any of these short-cut terms during the course of the reading, the copyholder will explain them in plain English. Speed should not be substituted for clarity.

TABLE 2-2. COPYHOLDER'S VOCABULARY—PUNCTUATION AND TYPE STYLE	
The Copyholder's Vocabulary	**Plain English**
one up, two up (etc.) (or) click	first-letter cap
three dots	ellipsis
four dots	ellipsis with period
bang	exclamation point
bold	boldface type
brack, close brack	bracket
caps (or) all-cap	all-capitalized words
cole	colon
com	comma
dent	indent
dent two (etc.)	indent two spaces or two ems
dot (or) stop	period
elsie (or) one down, two down	lowercase word

(cont.)

TABLE 2-2. (cont.)	
The Copyholder's Vocabulary	**Plain English**
em dash, en dash	length of dash
et	ampersand
huh (or) hey	question mark
hy (or) hook	hyphen
ital/end ital	italic type
new pare (or) graph	new paragraph
oh	the letter o
pos	apostrophe
pren, close pren	parenthesis
quote/unquote	quotation marks
rome	roman type
rule/end rule	underlined type
semi	semicolon
slash (or) slant	slash
snake	swung dash
spot	bullet
two hooks	two hyphens (as in "word-for-word")

TABLE 2-3. COPYHOLDER'S VOCABULARY—SYMBOLS AND NUMBERS	
The Copyholder's Vocabulary	**Plain English**
Symbols	
two balls	percent mark (%)
two dag	double dagger (‡)
ar mark	registration mark (®)
astrik	asterisk (*)
ball	degree mark (°)

(cont.)

TABLE 2-3. COPYHOLDER'S VOCABULARY—SYMBOLS AND NUMBERS (cont.)
buck . . . . .dollar symbol ($)
cee mark. . . . . .copyright mark (©)
cee slash. . . . . .cents symbol (¢)
dag . . . . .dagger (†)
star . . . . .star (★)
Numbers
hun . . . . .hundred (two zeros)
mil . . . . .million (six zeros)
num one, two (or) fig one, two. . . . . . .for numeral 12
point . . . . .decimal point
sub . . . . .inferior character
supe . . . . .superior character
thou. . . . . .thousand (three zeros)
twenty hy four. . . . . .twenty-four
zero . . . . .the numeral 0

3 PROOFREADING SKILLS

APTITUDE

There is a common misconception that anyone who can read, can proofread. But those who have accepted a job or have hired someone on that premise know better. There is literally more to it than meets the eye.

> According to management theory, our school system produces more ready-made proofreaders than there is a demand for. Only underpaid readers really believe this. The fact is that there is an aptitude requirement for reading, just as there is for music, mechanics or math.... Anyone with the capability and inclination to accept the discipline

of proofreading is a rare find. The fact is, a good proof-reader has an aptitude for reading.[2]

An aptitude for reading is, indeed, a prerequisite to good proofreading. Certainly one who doesn't like to read will not like to proofread. Even someone who enjoys reading may not enjoy proofreading *or* be good at it. There are other skills that the serious proofreader is motivated to develop and that supple-ment the natural inclinations one may possess (Table 3-1).

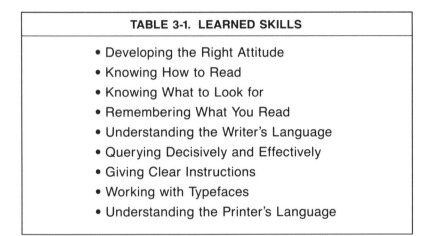

TABLE 3-1. LEARNED SKILLS

- Developing the Right Attitude
- Knowing How to Read
- Knowing What to Look for
- Remembering What You Read
- Understanding the Writer's Language
- Querying Decisively and Effectively
- Giving Clear Instructions
- Working with Typefaces
- Understanding the Printer's Language

DEVELOPING THE RIGHT ATTITUDE

Proofreading is a very intimidating and stressful occupation. Anyone who has ever done it knows why. The job requirements simply defy nature.

Hired to ensure perfect copy, the proofreader must catch everyone else's mistakes and not *make* one in the process. No matter whose error it might have been initially, the proofreader

---

[2] McNaughton, Harry H. *Proofreading & Copyediting.* New York: Hastings House, 1973.

is ultimately responsible. Unquestionably, anxiety comes with the territory. You should prepare yourself (and your ego) for the inevitable error, while at the same time do everything possible to avoid it.

Here are some ways to ease the tension while you read:

Clear the Room

You can't be sociable and proofread at the same time, so don't talk to others while you are trying to concentrate. Ringing telephones are another major nuisance. Even anticipating a telephone call will interfere with your ability to concentrate. A quiet place to work is essential to good proofreading.

Clear the Cobwebs

Fatigue or boredom creates distraction. If you are not totally focused on your work for either of these reasons, you will make errors. Count on it.

Fatigue.   Long copy or working hours don't necessarily condemn a reader to hours of unbroken concentration. Work breaks certainly help. And if you divide your work into segments, you will find it a much more productive approach.

Boredom.   Proofreading can be tedious when the copy is not interesting, when it is badly written, and especially when revisions of the same copy re-appear on your desk. But you can train yourself to be energetic and interested in whatever you are reading. If the copy isn't fascinating to read or doesn't offer an opportunity to learn, make it a challenge in another way. For example, make proofreading a game. Look for errors, and you are bound to find them. The subtle ones are just as important, and more fun and satisfying to catch, than the obvious ones. The more errors you know how to look for (in the language and in the type itself), the more you are going to find, and the more enjoyable and relaxed proofreading will be.

KNOWING HOW TO READ

Read the Instructions

You'll avoid numerous false starts, unnecessary questions, and mistakes if you read the instructions (if any) first. The writer or artist may have already anticipated your questions and included a guide for you. Try not to interrupt them with queries that have already been answered in the instructions. But if the information is confusing or unclear, do seek clarification before you begin the job.

Read Methodically

Always comparison read first—with a copyholder, a tape recorder, or alone—word for word at least once at each stage: typed, typeset, mechanical, and print. Then read the live copy again as many additional times as it takes to create your style sheet and to complete your tasks. When there is no dead text to compare, read the copy aloud, then read it again (and again) until you are confident that all errors have been found.

Read Slowly

People who are adept at speed-reading will never succeed at proofreading when those particular skills are employed. Read at a comfortable, deliberate pace. Don't allow a tight schedule or impatient co-workers to rush you. If you haven't the time to read the copy critically and slowly, wait until you do.

Read with Rhythm

Reading slowly doesn't always mean that you must read from letter to letter, unless that is the method you are most comfortable with. There are two exceptions: When you are reading very small or very large type and when you are reading foreign-language copy, you will have a much better chance of catching all the mistakes if you stop to look carefully at each letter.

Neither do you have to read from word to word, once the first-time comparison reading has been completed. The pace of subsequent readings can accelerate to a moderate speed through a series of eye stops across a line of print. The eye moves along, stops to let in the light needed to see an image, then moves on to the next eye stop. With practice, you can see two, sometimes three words per eye stop, depending of course on the length of the word.

First focus your eyes on one word, the whole word, if possible. Then try two. Find the most comfortable span for your eyes, and practice reading this way. Your vision should flow, not jump, from one eye stop to the next. Keep the rhythm of the flow to the end of the line.

If your eye span is too short to take in an entire word or two, practice reading by word syllables. Expanding your eye stops will automatically produce speed. More importantly, it will produce a steadier rhythm.

Contrary to what some occasional proofreaders believe, reading the copy backward is unnecessary torture and, if you are a full-time proofreader, a painful way to earn a living. Many proofreaders who insist on this method eventually disappear from the trade altogether.

Look for Red Flags

Reading methodically, slowly, and with rhythm works most of the time. But there are some places in the copy that should send warning signals for an even closer look:

▶ copy that *you* have written or typed

▶ revised copy

▶ long lines of type

▶ short lines of type

▶ double consonants or vowels

▶ a series of thin letters (*ili, ifi,* and *til*)

▶ all-capitalized letters or large, headline type

▶ black letter or ornamental type

▶ sans serif type

▶ italicized letters

▶ numerals: decimal points, commas, alignment, totals

▶ pairs of parentheses, quote marks, brackets, dashes

KNOWING WHAT TO LOOK FOR

It is a long journey between the original text and the printed word, and there are many proofreading hazards every step of the way. Remembering all the different kinds of errors you are looking for (and finding them all in the short amount of time you will have to read) takes experience.

Proofreading Checklists

The wise beginner will categorize those duties in a logical order, then separate them by readings. You will need four lists, one for every stage of production (Appendix B). You won't need the lists forever, but refer to them for as long as you do. Soon the routine should become second-nature.

The suggested lists may be insufficient or excessive or not in your preferred grouping. That will depend on the nature of the copy you are reading and the limit of your responsibility and authority. You may want to combine some of the readings or divide them even further, with one exception. Even the pros—especially the pros—separate mechanical (format) tasks from reading tasks. You don't have to confine your readings to a certain number of passes. Just read until you feel the job is done.

Following the list as you read, you will undoubtedly spot errors you are not looking for at that particular reading. Mark them *when* you see them. Do not wait until you are scheduled to, because you might then overlook them.

Look now at the checklists (Appendix B) for reading typed copy, typeset copy, the mechanical, and the printer's proof.

Common Errors

You also might want to keep a list of the most common errors that can occur:

▶ incorrectly spelled names

▶ reversed numbers in addresses

▶ incorrect dates

▶ incorrect capitalization

▶ doubly typed words or phrases

▶ omissions of words or parts of words

▶ incorrect or deleted punctuation

▶ nonagreement of subject and verb

▶ misspelled words

Other Tips

▶ Sometimes when you find one error, you may find a whole nest of them nearby.

▶ Errors that recur just could be intentional spellings or usages, so ask before you begin making unnecessary corrections.

▶ Watch for words that are commonly misused or misspelled or sound alike but have different meanings (Appendix C).

▶ Watch for changes in typeface or type size.

▶ Make sure bibliography entries are alphabetical, that authors' names and titles are spelled correctly, that the information is in proper order and is punctuated correctly. Bibliographies should be carefully proofread against the original text.

▶ Check titles, subtitles, charts, and page numbers against the table of contents and index. Check any references to page numbers within the text, making sure they correspond to the reference material.

4 REMEMBERING WHAT YOU READ

Proofreading is never a routine occupation. Even during a second or third pass, you will inevitably discover some error or inconsistency that you missed the first time around. Keep alert, and you will eliminate some of those repeated readings. Concentrate, and you will remember much of what you have read.

While it's necessary to cultivate a good memory for detail, inconsistencies, and repetition, you don't have to remember everything. Just know where to find what you are looking for. A stylebook or style sheet is one of the best reminders a proofreader can have. This has nothing to do with literary style. It's a set of rules or guidelines intended to ensure consistency of format, spelling, capitalization, abbreviations, word usage, and other technicalities peculiar to the language and to the copy you are reading.

THE STYLEBOOK

Published stylebooks are commercially available and are excellent resources for general office use. Designed for a specific group of writers and editors (and proofreaders), their popularity has quickly spread beyond the particular community for which they were originally intended.

For example, *The New York Times* mandates style standards that must be followed by all of its writers. So does the U.S. government in its stylebook. And the University of Chicago *Manual of Style* has long been a respected source of style for academic writers. There are many other such publications, varying in content and emphasis, and one of them will likely be appropriate for your office.

Editors usually decide what stylebook will be used or they will set a style themselves. In an office where there is no editor or book or style to follow, the proofreader should request one, be permitted to choose or develop a standard, or create a style sheet that follows the predominant style, assuming it is a correct one, of the copy being read.

THE STYLE SHEET

The style sheet is not a random listing of points to be remembered while reading the copy. It is much more calculated and organized than that. Otherwise, you will not easily find the information without searching through the entire list each time. You could spend as much (or more) time searching for style as you would reading the copy. The right kind of style sheet is intended to save time and trouble. Know what points of style to look for (Table 4-1), faithfully maintain a style sheet that reflects the style of the copy you are reading, and refer to the style sheet as often as you need to.

TABLE 4-1. POINTS OF STYLE
• Format
• Spelling and capitalization
• Hyphenations
• Numerals
• Plurals, possessives, and punctuation
• Abbreviations
• Special treatment
• Dates
• Foreign words
• Facts
• Trademarks and service marks, copyrights, and logotypes
• Footnotes, bibliographies, and tables
• Miscellaneous

Format

If the physical appearance (layout) of the copy has not already been specified, either through office policy or by the editor or artist, format will be identified by glancing through the copy, measuring its dimensions, and writing them down on the style sheet. For future reference, attach to the style sheet samples of work—memos, conference reports, business letters, manuscripts, newsletters, or any other copy formats that will be referred to again. Seeing how the copy should actually look is much easier than having to calculate dimensions each time. (See Table 4-2.)

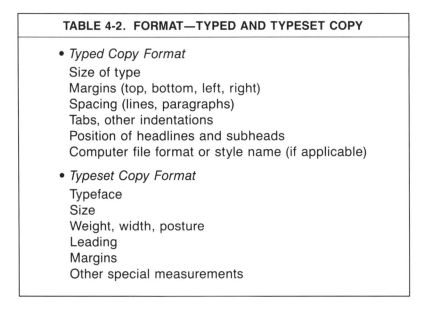

TABLE 4-2. FORMAT—TYPED AND TYPESET COPY

- *Typed Copy Format*
  Size of type
  Margins (top, bottom, left, right)
  Spacing (lines, paragraphs)
  Tabs, other indentations
  Position of headlines and subheads
  Computer file format or style name (if applicable)

- *Typeset Copy Format*
  Typeface
  Size
  Weight, width, posture
  Leading
  Margins
  Other special measurements

Spelling and Capitalization

It is important that you include on the style sheet the exact spelling and capitalization of proper nouns (names, places, organizations), noting carefully anything unusual. For example, if it's *Mr. Jonathan Smythe* you are reading about in the copy, make sure he doesn't become *Mr. John Smith* later in the copy. And if you first read, then record, *U.S. Postal Service* (after making sure it was the proper usage), you will know that *U.S. Post Office* or *post office,* which may appear later in the copy, should be changed or at least questioned. If *The Citizens and Southern National Bank* (note the cap *T* and lowercase *and*) is referred to again but this time as *the C&S Bank* (note lowercase *t* and *&*), either reference may be correct. You will remember the details if they are written in the style sheet. You will also know what to do if *C&S* later appears as *C & S* (note spacing).

To avoid having to search through the copy each time you see an inconsistency, first determine the proper spelling or capitalization or spacing (by asking the editor, finding the answer yourself, or using the predominant style). Then write it down legibly in the appropriate box on your style sheet. You will have to look no further than your style sheet the next time you have a style question.

Another important point to remember is that sometimes words may be spelled two ways (*toward/towards, data base/database*). Dictionaries often list a preference. According to *The American Heritage Dictionary* (Second College Edition), "*judgment also judgement*" (note *also*) are both generally accepted but the first spelling is preferred; and although both "*ax or axe*" (note *or*) are accepted, there is no preference of one over the other. (Be sure to consult the guide in the dictionary you are using. Some may indicate a preference differently.) When there is no preference, it is the writer's or editor's choice. Get into the habit of looking for, or asking about, these special words.

Hyphenations

Often words are hyphenated when used either as compound adjectives or compound nouns (*full-service* [adj] or *decision-maker* [n]) but are not hyphenated when they are used together as an adjective and noun (*full service, decision maker*). If you get confused or if the copy isn't consistent, ask the editor or writer. Some like hyphens, some don't. Or follow the predominant style.

List on the style sheet all compound words that have potential for creating hyphenation problems for you later on. The list will be especially helpful if you are reading long copy.

Hyphens can create confusion in other ways, such as when the first letters of all headline words are capitalized (called initial caps) and one of those words is hyphenated. The word before the hyphen is capitalized, but what about the word following the hyphen? *By-pass This Street*? Or *By-Pass This Street*? The editor or artist may choose to initial-cap *Pass*, because it looks better that way.

Another decision must be made when similar words are used in a series and the dictionary recognizes some of them as hyphenated words and some as complete words:

> The writer must *re-read* and *rewrite*, or *replace,* the copy and *re-position* it on the page.

This creates a visually unattractive line and it often becomes a style decision, rather than a matter of correct hyphenation, to avoid creating undue attention. The editor will choose either to hyphenate all of them or, most likely, to eliminate the hyphens altogether and close up the space after the prefix.

There are many such decisions that will be made based on style rather than correctness. Although you will not make these decisions, at least make a mental note of them. You will feel much more comfortable knowing why rules are sometimes broken. And soon you will be able to recognize and point out potential troublemakers such as these.

Numerals

There is no single, official rule or style for writing numerals, although there are some commonly preferred ones among those who write or publish for a living.

Numerical tables and columns of numbers are usually expressed in digits. When numbers appear randomly throughout the copy, most journalists use a standardized style of writing out as words the numbers *one* through *nine*, and as figures from *10* on. An accepted variation of this is spelling out *one* through *ninety-nine*, then using numerical figures from *100* on. The writer or editor may choose one of these styles, use all digits, or spell them all—whichever style looks best and appropriate for a particular piece of copy.

Watch for inconsistent treatment of numbers used mone-
tarily (such as *10¢, $.10, ten cents, 10 cents*) and make sure they
are all treated uniformly. A style should also be determined for
percentages (ten percent, 10%, and so on).

Plurals, Possessives, and Punctuation

There are grammatical rules that help the writer or editor decide
how to treat plural and possessive words. (In advertising copy,
the writer may also be guided by client preference. See Special
Treatment, page 33.) There is sometimes a choice of style, however, and you should know the rules well enough to keep up the
consistency throughout the reading. Here are a few examples of
plural and possessive treatment:

Letters: L's; also Ls
a's, e's, i's, not as, es, is
A's, E's, I's, not As, Es, Is

Words: if's, and's, or but's; also ifs, ands, or buts
miss's, not misss; do's and don'ts, not dos or
don't's
Davis's house; also Davis' house
Chris's money, but Chris' salary
Joe's and Jane's cars
Joe and Jane's car; also Joe's and Jane's car

Figures: 7's or 7s

Symbols: &'s or &s

Acronyms: UFO's or UFOs; Ph.D.'s, not Ph.D.s

Dates: 1800's or 1800s

Punctuation is editorial territory, but the more familiar you
are with the rules, the better able you will be to spot an error
when you see one. Except for a few choices (such as hyphenation, the use of the apostrophe as shown above, or adding a

comma after an introductory phrase or before a conjunction in a series), there is no punctuation "style." Copy is either punctuated right or punctuated wrong. And most writers or editors will not take too many liberties with the rules if they want to be understood. Making sure that punctuation is exactly as they want it is your job. Understanding why makes the job more enjoyable.

Abbreviations

Abbreviations are not always treated consistently by writers. And that can be a problem for the proofreader. The best advice is to look up the abbreviation in either a good dictionary or a published stylebook, then write it down in the appropriate alphabetized box on your style sheet. Sometimes there is more than one way to abbreviate a word or group of words. In the absence of an editor, the proofreader chooses the most common style evident in the copy and uses it as the guide for all abbreviations. Some examples follow:

> States: Conn. or CT, Neb. or NE, N.Y. or NY
> Direction: N.W., NW, or NW.
> Degrees: Ph.D., A.B., B.S., M.B.A., not PhD, AB, BS, MBA
> Times of Day: A.M., A.M., or a.m.; P.M., P.M., or p.m.
> Titles: C.P.A. or CPA, F.B.I. or FBI

Some abbreviations are not so straightforward. Abbreviations for some common nouns, such as *public service announcement (PSA)*, *physical education (PE)*, or *account executive (AE)* are capitalized, while others, such as for *government (gov. or govt.)* and *afternoon (aft.)* are lowercase. Watch the caps and the periods. Look them up and monitor use carefully.

There are still other abbreviated words to watch out for, words the average reader (but not the average proofreader) may fail to notice. The nonword *'til* is often used as an abbreviation of *until*. Experts still agree that the correct abbreviation is *till*, no matter how illogical it may appear. Look at the different abbreviations for the word *and*: *'n, n', or 'n'*. In most cases, the most accepted rule is to use an apostrophe whenever and wherever a letter or letters are omitted.

An abbreviation that should be questioned by the proofreader is the use of a dash (—) or the nonword *thru* for *through*. And a dash (—) or ellipsis (...) is often incorrectly used as a substitute for commas, semicolons, or end marks. This is especially common in advertising copy. But most proofreaders don't get too entangled in enforcing these rules if they are not important to the editor. Cite the rule (and the reference), then follow the editor's decision consistently throughout.

Special Treatment

If the end justifies the means, any writer may deliberately deviate from commonly accepted style, spell a word differently than it appears in the dictionary, capitalize an ordinarily lowercase word or lowercase a traditionally capitalized word, make up new words, deviate from rules of grammar and punctuation, or do anything else that will make the copy unique. Special treatment is quite evident in advertising copy as an attention-getting device or simply because the client wants it that way (Table 4-3). If you must work with this kind of copy on a day-to-day basis, get familiar with the deviations. And if you can't remember all of them, let the style sheet do it for you.

TABLE 4-3. ADVERTISING DEVIATIONS FROM SPELLING OR GRAMMAR[3]

American Express® Travelers Cheques

Winston® Tastes Good Like A Cigarette Should

Diet-Rite® Cola

Kwik Koting®

More cheesier (Kraft Macaroni & Cheese Dinner)

BTU-tiful™

UnflappaBull (Bull Worldwide Information Systems)

Dr Pepper®

Heat'N'Serve®

Dates

Dates may be written in a variety of styles, so find the most prevalent one, ask the editor, or establish one yourself. Any of the following styles are acceptable; all you have to do is ensure consistency.

▶ 18th century or eighteenth century (adjective and noun)

▶ 18th-century or eighteenth-century (compound adjective)

▶ 1900's or 1900s

▶ October 1989; October, 1989; Oct. 1989; Oct., 1989; 10/89

---

[3] Travelers Cheques is a trademark of American Express Travel Related Services Company, Inc. Winston is a registered trademark of the Reynolds Tobacco Company. Diet-Rite is a registered trademark of Royal Crown Cola Co. Kwik Koting is a trademark of the Martin Varnish Co. "More cheesier" is a term used by Kraft, Inc. BTU-tiful is a registered trademark of the American Gas Association. UnflappaBull is used by the Bull HN Information Systems Inc. Dr Pepper is a trademark of the Dr Pepper Company. Heat'N'Serve is a trademark of Sunbeam Appliance Co.

▶ January 10, 1976; 10 January 1976; Jan. 10, 1976; 10 Jan. 1976; 01/10/76 (preferred over 1/10/76). Americans don't use 10/01/76 when the date is January 10, 1976. The informal January '76 may be used only when it is not accompanied by a day (don't use January 10, '76).

Remember, if a comma precedes the year, another comma must follow if it is not at the end of a sentence. Example: "His first book was published June 1, 1988, and was a best-seller." but "His first book was published June 1988 and was a best-seller."

Foreign Words

It is rare that copy written in English will contain more than a scattering of foreign words or phrases. List all that are used in the copy, noting accent marks and their positioning over or under the words. Americans are not accustomed to accent marks and occasionally will put them in the wrong place or at the wrong angle or neglect them altogether. They *are* relevant. All foreign words (except those commonly adopted by Americans, such as "avant-garde" or "hors d'oeuvre") should be italicized or underscored.

Facts

In many jobs that you read, the subject matter will not be familiar to you. And in long manuscripts, it is difficult to remember or record all the facts stated. It isn't as hard remembering the facts in advertising copy, especially if the client (and you) have been with the agency for a long time.

Although the proofreader is not usually liable for any factual misinformation and inconsistencies, your careful attention to detail would be welcomed by all. Write down on your style sheet what facts you do learn from reading the copy. As an experienced proofreader you will develop almost a second sense for those facts you will most likely need to remember. An example in advertising copy: "...fourteen offices throughout the city" followed by a list of only twelve addresses later in the copy or even in another advertisement.

Trademarks and Service Marks

In any nonfictional copy, watch for trademarks (^{TM}), service marks (^{SM}), and registration marks (®) and list them beside the product name in the style sheet. One mark cannot be substituted for another mark.

The Trademark Act of 1946 defines a trademark as follows:

> The term "trademark" includes any word, name, symbol, or device or any combination thereof adopted and used by a manufacturer or merchant to identify his goods and distinguish them from those manufactured by others. (15 U.S.C. 1127)

The Trademark Act of 1946 defines a service mark as follows:

> The term "service mark" means a mark used in the sale or advertising of services to identify the services of one person and distinguish them from the services of others. (15 U.S.C. 1127)

If either a trademark or service mark is registered in the U.S. Patent and Trademark Office, the 1946 Trademark Act requires that it must be followed by one of three forms of notice:

1. Registered in U.S. Patent and Trademark Office.

2. Reg. U.S. Pat. & Tm. Off.

3. ®

The ® is most often used as notice of a mark's registration. If a mark isn't registered in the U.S. Patent and Trademark Office, it is protected under common law of the states when one of the following common law marks is used:

1. ™ (a common law mark that is a trademark)

2. ˢᴹ (a common law mark that is a service mark)

A common law mark may become registered in the U.S. Patent and Trademark Office. When that happens, the ™ or the ˢᴹ will become ®.

These marks are public, legal notices to the reader that the company wants to protect its product and service names from encroachment by another company. If the marks aren't used consistently in advertisements or in other communications (even internal communications), or if the company doesn't take steps to preserve those rights when others use the name without permission, those rights could be lost and the product or service name could become a generic term and, consequently, common property of anyone who wants to use it.

In advertising copy, names of products belonging to the client will usually bear one of these marks to identify ownership. Unless specifically instructed to do otherwise, you should make sure that a mark follows the product name once per page, usually at first mention or most prominent position. Sometimes, too, depending on client preference, a footnote appears at the bottom of the page or at the end of the copy as an additional means of identifying the product owner.

Products or services that are the property of a company other than your client are sometimes discussed in the advertisement as well. They must be similarly marked in the copy and always identified in a footnote.

The common procedure to footnote a product that is a registered trademark:

Widget is a registered trademark of the ABC Company.

As a trademark or service mark will be positioned beside the name Widget in the body of the copy, it is not necessary to place another registration mark beside it in the footnote.

Company names also may be registered as trade names (not marks) and are accompanied by a registration mark if they are used as adjectives modifying a word that describes a type of product or service. Used alone, as nouns, a company name does not require a mark notice, unless it is used with the registered logotype. For example, when the company name American Express is used alone, as a noun, it is not followed by a registration mark. When it is used as an adjective modifying one of its products or services, it is followed by a registration mark (American Express® Travelers Cheques). And when it appears beside the logo (usually at the bottom of the advertisement), it will most likely be accompanied by a registration or common law mark.

Copyright Marks

Another footnote line is standard on all published copy to protect it from being used in any way without permission of the copyright owner. Copyright lines are included in all books, magazine articles and brochures, and most advertisements. The date of the copyright is the date the article was first published. If the copy is changed or altered in any way, it becomes "new copy" and the copyright must be updated accordingly to reflect the new material. The proofreader should remember to check the inclusion of a copyright and make sure the date and name are correct.

©1989 ABC Company **or** Copyright (or Copr.) 1989 ABC Company

A trademark or service mark that fits the definition of a "work" under the Copyright Act may also be copyrighted. Some foreign countries do not recognize marks other than the copyright mark, so it is used for protection against international infringement.

Logotypes

The corporate logo is commonly used on any printed material that is published by a corporation or by an advertising agency on behalf of its client. Often registered in the U.S. Patent and Trademark Office, the logo consists of the corporate name and a corporate symbol (both usually in a special typeface and design). It is positioned somewhere on the page or advertisement, usually at the bottom, ahead of the legal footnotes. Logos are carefully designed to create a visual image of the corporation, one that a casual reader of the advertisement will remember long after the words in the advertisement have been forgotten. Logos and their accompanying registration mark are an essential item in the proofreader's style sheet and on the proofreader's checklist.

Footnotes, Bibliographies, and Tables

You will follow the style set by the writer or editor. Write at least one example of each in the style sheet and refer to the examples for style and consistency.

Miscellaneous

There will often be points that you will want to remember but cannot categorize in your style sheet: facts, addresses, phone numbers, scientific or legal terms, and so on. A "Miscellaneous" box will serve as a catchall for those odds and ends that you may need to compare as you progress through the copy.

You may not use all the suggested points of style in some copy you will be reading. Or you may want to add a few new ones to the style sheet you compile for other jobs. Design or modify your style sheet so that it will accommodate you and the copy you are reading. Alphabetize the points in each box.

DESIGNING YOUR STYLE SHEET

Take several sheets of paper, preferably $8^1/_2'' \times 11''$ for easy handling, distributing, and filing. You are going to alphabetize items, so draw or type enough boxes on the sheets to include each letter of the alphabet (X, Y, and Z items can usually fit into one box). Draw some additional boxes for points that can't be alphabetized (punctuation and style, footnotes and references, special symbols, treatment of numerals, typing format, and typographic style). See Table 4-4 for an example.

For some proofreading jobs, the narrow ruled boxes may not provide sufficient space to record all the points you need to remember. You may feel less confined with ruled lines that extend the full width of the page (Table 4-5).

General Office Style Sheet

The simplest style sheet is a compilation of predetermined general standards by which every piece of written or typed copy emanating from the office is compared. This includes memos, business correspondence, annual reports, and everything in between. You may want a separate style sheet for each. The wide box style sheet may be more suitable for these points than the narrow box style sheet. (See Appendix D.)

TABLE 4-4. NARROW BOX STYLE SHEET		
Trademarks Registration Marks Service Marks Logos Copyrights Other Legal	Typing Format	Type Specifications

Special Usage/
    Placement
	Numerical Style	Miscellaneous
		    Facts/Notes

TABLE 4-4. *(cont.)*		
Capitalization **Hyphenation** **Italics Marks** **Possessives** **Punctuation** **Spelling** (adj) adjective (cn) collective noun (dict) dictionary preference (n) noun (pa) predicate adj. (pl) plural (poss) possessive (sing) singular (v) verb	A	B
C	D	E
F	G	H (and so on)

TABLE 4-5. WIDE BOX STYLE SHEET
Trademarks/Logos
Registration Marks/Legal
Special Usage/Placement
Typing Format
Type Specifications
Numerical Style

TABLE 4-5. *(cont.)*
Capitalization/Hyphenation/Italics/Possessive/ Punctuation/Spelling
(adj) adjective   (pl) plural (cn) collective noun   (poss) possessive (dict) dictionary preference (sing) singular (n) noun   (v) verb (pa) predicate adj.
A
B
C (and so on)
Footnotes, Bibliographies, and Tables
Miscellaneous Facts/Notes

The style sheet(s) can be sketchy or elaborately detailed, but it should include the basics such as format instructions, spacing, capitalization, special punctuation, treatment of numerals, spelling of frequently used words such as proper nouns—in short, whatever should be considered blanket office policy. Organized by subject matter, this style sheet should be typed and distributed to every employee. Additions, deletions, and any changes should be made promptly and re-circulated to office workers.

Manuscript Style Sheet

Another kind of style sheet is primarily used for book manuscripts or any copy that, as far as the proofreader is aware, has no predetermined editorial style. It is created during the actual reading. (See Appendix E.)

Except in unusual circumstances, the proofreader will not set style in the same manner as an editor would. You will instead identify the style that most often recurs in the text, then begin compiling the style sheet accordingly.

Once style has been established and recorded on the style sheet, everyone who subsequently works with the copy should follow it and be informed when any style changes occur.

How To Begin.   Start listing points on your style sheet during the second reading, not the first. The reasons: If your first pass is one of comparison reading, it will be too disruptive to you (and to the copyholder) if you must stop to make periodic style sheet entries at the same time you are comparing dead and live copy. Also, once you have read the copy, you will have a clearer understanding of the content. This makes it easier to determine what the style point is or what it should be.

As you read, begin writing down each point, as you come to it, in the appropriate box. Try to remember (from the first reading) whether that point is repeated in the manuscript. Even if you don't remember it recurring in the text, but it looks as though it might be useful later, write it down on the style sheet.

As soon as a different usage of the same point appears in the text, and if there is no previously determined style, make (or get) a decision on style treatment before you read further. You don't want to have to search through the entire document to find and change them all. Use the same style for all similar points.

For the sake of speed, the style sheet need not be typed, especially if it will be used only by you for that single manuscript. But if the same subject and style will be used in subsequent assignments and especially if the style sheet will be followed by co-workers, an eventual typing of the guide will make it easier for everyone.

Client Style Sheet

In advertising agencies client style sheets are compiled in a similar fashion, except there most likely will be a few pre-existing rules coming from the client before copy writing, even conception, actually begins. (See Appendix F.)

A style sheet for client copy is usually referred to repeatedly over time by writers, typists, and proofreaders. Once style has been established, it should be typed and distributed to office personnel who work with the client. A copy should also be given to the client for information and approval. Separate style sheets are maintained for each client. They are minutely detailed, as are manuscript style sheets.

An agency usually has many different clients. Those clients have products with different "personalities." And so will the ads created for them. Copy language may be formal and business-like for a bank client, casual and playful for a client who owns a pizza parlor. Typeface and layout design will be chosen accordingly by the artist.

Clients may have additional copy style preferences. One client may use a comma between its corporate name and the word "Inc." Another client may not. One may capitalize, even spell, certain key words in ways not ordinarily recognized by a dictionary. Some clients may want a registration mark after every mention of their product names; others may require only one registration mark per page. Some want copyright lines and other legal footnotes at the bottom of their ads; others don't. Trade names used as possessives are not allowed by many clients; product names used as adjectives or as nouns may also be forbidden. Client preferences are often too numerous to remember and always too important to forget. So keep a list of them.

How To Begin.   Client style and product information emanate from the client to the account executive, who passes it along to the copywriter. The copywriter, the artist, and occasionally the creative director will create the ad.

The proofreader is usually the custodian of the original style sheet, compiling it while proofreading the ad copy. You should make sure that the style sheet reflects the exact style designed by the creative team, that everyone on the team always has an updated version of it, and that it is followed precisely in each advertisement. When style deviations or changes occur, the proofreader will consult with the writer or account executive for a decision, then notify all others involved with the client account of subsequent changes in style.

Most client style sheets evolve as the ad campaign progresses. There will most likely be some additions, deletions, and changes in style during the next campaign. Keeping them current and enforcing the rules is one of the hardest and most important challenges of the proofreader. One deviation could lead to another, and the style would become a useless collection of contradictory rules. Inconsistency can destroy otherwise good ad copy, not to mention friendly client-agency relationships.

5 UNDERSTANDING THE WRITER'S LANGUAGE AND QUERYING EFFECTIVELY

The writer's craft is the proofreader's as well. And the most valuable resource a writer can have is a proofreader who knows the language and the mechanics that make it work.

There is a certain flexibility or permissiveness unique to the American-English language. We often make one word where there used to be two; we change nouns to verbs and adjectives to nouns. We alter the meanings, even create new words when the old ones seem inadequate.

STUDY IT

A word can be misused for such a long time that its correct usage begins to sound awkward. Meanwhile, some dictionaries—

at least those with a penchant to bend established order to accommodate popular usage—have made its misuses officially acceptable.

The question then raised is whose rules to follow? The purist can become hopelessly entangled in and frustrated by conflicting viewpoints of language experts, and the result can be a total inability to make any firm commitment. Indecision can break the best of proofreaders. But so can rigidity.

Efforts to resolve this issue concerning the language have been documented as far back as 200 years. James Adams's idea of "refining, correcting, improving, and ascertaining the English language" was squelched by Thomas Jefferson: ". . . Judicious neology [the coining of a new word, phrase, or expression from conversation] can alone give strength and copiousness to language, and enable it to be the vehicle of new ideas,"[4] reflected Mr. Jefferson. No resolution followed.

Nevertheless, this war over words continues even today between the progressive and the dogmatic. In the opening pages of *The American Heritage Dictionary*, two well-known writers present opposing views in an essay titled "The Prevailing Usage of Its Speakers Should Be the Chief Determinant of the Language." No resolution follows.

So without anyone to settle the debate, our language continues to grow, changing faster than any language in the world. And the proofreader must keep pace by developing an extraordinary curiosity and sensitivity to the flow.

If reading is one of your major means of outside entertainment (as it is for many proofreaders), you will find it a source for many new words to add to your vocabulary. Study Words and Phrases Commonly Confused or Misused (Appendix C). Or create your own list of troublemakers and keep them close by.

---

[4] *The American Heritage Dictionary,* Second College Edition, Boston: Houghton Mifflin Company, 1985.

A good dictionary is the most valuable resource a proof-reader can have. There is a wealth of information few people ever bother to consider, or even know is included! Learn how to use it by studying the guide in the foreword. There you will find the key to word meanings and pronunciations, and words or expressions unique to a specific region or unacceptable (nonstandard) anywhere. You will also learn how to find idioms, colloquialisms, parts of speech, verb tenses, antonyms, homonyms, abbreviations, even examples of sentences in which the word is used. Signs, symbols, measurement tables, geographic and biographical entries, proofreading symbols—the list goes on. Dictionaries are the proofreader's best friend. Keep your dictionary close by whenever and wherever you read.

There will always be dictionaries and other reference books that accept what you might consider a suspect word or definition faster than you do. If it is sanctioned by a reputable source, the writer has a justifiable claim to it. If it is not approved on good authority, it is a point of concern and should be flagged by the proofreader.

The conversational and the written word also have recognized differences. Written copy is more formal; the language should not be corrupted, as it frequently—and unfortunately—is in dialogue.

S-P-E-L-L IT RIGHT

Good spellers are usually born, not made. If learning to spell comes hard, so will recognizing a misspelled word. Certain words will stump the best of spellers. And if you can't remember them, it's not a blemish on your reputation if you have to look them up and store them in your style sheet for future reference.

The spelling check in some computer word processing programs should eliminate most of the misspellings before the proofreader sees the copy, but it won't catch everything. It won't catch a word that is spelled correctly but in the wrong place. It also cannot distinguish between a right word and a wrong word if both are spelled correctly. If "from" was typed when "form" was meant, the computer won't find an error, but a proofreader who understands context—and knows how to spell—will.

Incorrect word breaks are another mistake a good proofreader just doesn't allow to happen. Words that are spelled the same but have two different meanings may also be divided differently (pre-sent [v]; pres-ent [n]). Learn the rules for determining syllables and, when in doubt, look it up.

How do you find a word in the dictionary if you can't spell it? Look it up the way it sounds. If you can't find it there, try another combination of letters with the same sound. Learning how a word is pronounced may also help you spell it correctly.

When looking up words, read the entire definition. Some words have variant meanings and pronunciations, as well as different spellings and syllable breaks. Either variant may be acceptable, or there may be an official preference. British spellings, often side-by-side with American spellings, should not be used in the United States.

PARLEZ-VOUS...?

Unless you are fluent, proofreading foreign languages, even occasional phrases, can be tricky. A Spanish word can convey one meaning to a Miami reader, a different meaning to a reader in Texas. Proofreaders who don't know the language well should not look for anything other than typographical errors, assuming the original copy is correct.

KNOW THE MECHANICS

Extraordinary as it may seem, many writers do not know, much less use correctly, the tools of their own trade. Grammar and punctuation make the language work, and the proofreader's knowledge of both is vital. For most of us, formal study of the mechanics doesn't extend beyond high school. If memories of it are dim, take a refresher course or dig out your old textbook (or your dictionary), study it, and refer to it as often as you need to. You may be the only grammatical lifeline between the typed copy and the published word.

There are many good grammar and punctuation books on the market, in both college and commercial bookstores. Although the content in all of them is primarily the same, examine each before you buy and choose one that is easy to read, clear in explanation, and thorough.

WHEN TO QUERY

Don't be afraid to ask questions. If something about the copy looks wrong, query it. (See Table 5-1.) You should never be embarrassed about asking questions. You may learn from them. It is those questions you don't ask that can come back to haunt you. Querying decisively means asking questions but using good judgment at the same time.

TABLE 5-1. POINTS OF QUERY
• Subject and verb agreement
• Incorrect grammar or word usage
• Punctuation inconsistency
• Factual inaccuracy or inconsistency
• Contradiction or repetition
• Clarity or meaning

Good writing deserves good proofreading; bad writing demands it. More often than writers like to admit, they make errors: grammatical, punctuation, misspellings, awkward phrasing, even factual. A good proofreader feels accountable for every one of these errors.

Just how much responsibility should you as a proofreader try to assume? Short of rewriting the copy and making needless changes, just as much as you are capable of. It is your duty to catch, or at least query, everything you think is wrong, no matter whose formal responsibility it may be. But you must be as informed as you can be of the point in question and approach with great caution any error that is outside your assigned duties.

As has been repeated throughout this book, there is sometimes a thin line between proofreading and copyediting. Make sure you know the difference. Correcting copy is the proofreader's job. Changing copy is the editor's (or writer's).

WHAT TO QUERY

Proofreaders shouldn't extend their questions into what is the editor's or writer's domain, such as badly written sentences. If you think a sentence needs a closer look, you should point out something specifically wrong (such as a comma splice or a dangling phrase) or confusing (such as a change of tense).

Don't ask idle questions about problems you haven't already researched. While you will learn plenty on the job, most of what you learn should result from your own study and observation; neither the editor nor the writer has the time (or probably the inclination) to teach you. Whatever you query, do it carefully and thoughtfully.

Correcting mistakes or querying what you believe is an error always calls for diplomacy and, in some instances, persuasive strategy. If it was obvious that the writer didn't know better, cite or attach rules from authoritative sources. This says to the writer that you gave intelligent thought to the problem and that you didn't make up the rule (you will often be challenged, if you don't). While this helps the writer understand and learn from mistakes, it also helps the writer decide whether to break or bend the rules.

When a rule is broken or if the writer disagrees with one of your corrections, you need to understand why. Discuss it when you both have the opportunity. You may learn something. To correct or not is the writer's (or editor's) choice. And even if you think it is the wrong choice, you must learn to live with that particular limitation of the proofreader's role.

Some writers are resistant to any suggestions, and the proofreader must learn to live with that, as well. Under all circumstances, remember that the proofreader is the writer's ally and support, not competition. Building trust between yourself and the writer is essential to the success of the assignment, as well as to your own success as an effective proofreader.

HOW TO QUERY

The easiest way is to circle the word or words in question. In the margin write a question mark and circle it, or write out *okay?* and circle it. (The circled mark in the margin indicates only an instruction or question; if you don't circle it, this implies that you want the mark typed or typeset.)

The circled query mark, alone in the margin, can place a burden on the editor or writer, who must try to guess why the word or words caused you concern. What confused *you* may not be a quickly evident to *them*. You'll get quicker results if you write out your question.

If your query is ignored, it may have been overlooked or not understood. Restate your question and send it back to the person who can answer the question. Write out what problem you think the word has created or the rule that you think may have been broken. This gives the writer full information and a choice of solving the problem or leaving it alone.

Another way to ask questions is by making a query list as you read, noting the page number and line number, and writing down the specific questions you may have. The separate query list (or, with the list in hand, a conversation with the writer or editor) is the only method available to you when you are correcting copy from most computer terminals. Writing down your questions is also a good way to query when you are reading long copy. Answers to questions you initially may have could become evident as you get further into the copy, and a query won't be necessary by the time you reach the end of the job.

Those who proofread for typesetters or printers must handle corrections and queries quite differently than those proofreaders in editorial or other business offices. The writer isn't around to talk with. And your company's policy is usually firm: Do not change the customer's copy. If it is a simple spelling or grammatical error—and you must be absolutely sure that it is an error—make the change (but always with a notation to the customer). Or ask the typesetter to "chunk" the correction. Chunk means to reset that word or line of copy with your correction, and place it at the bottom of the typeset page. This gives the customer an opportunity to see it both as originally written and as corrected by you. Don't get too involved with customer copy except, of course, to correct the typesetter's mistakes. It is time-consuming, it is beyond your area of responsibility, and it could alienate the customer.

6 GIVING CLEAR INSTRUCTIONS

PROOFREADER'S MARKS

The proofreader's marks (Table 6-1) are shorthand symbols that everyone in the trade understands and uses. While they may look like a foreign language, close study will reveal logic and simplicity. One proof mark will often substitute for many words and will be instantly recognized by anyone working with the copy.

Although most symbols are standard throughout the communication industry, you will discover a few variations from office to office if you are in the business long enough. You may want to adapt to them or request that your coworkers conform to yours. Either way, standardizing the marks officewide avoids confusion. The main objective is getting the message across clearly and quickly.

The proofreader's marks are a vital link of communication among the members of the creative team. They also transmit the same important information to the typesetter and printer.

HOW TO MAKE THE MARKS

Copy corrections must be conveyed as neatly and concisely as possible. Use an indelible-ink pen on typing paper or a reader's proof (the color red is easiest to see), a nonreproducing pen on camera-ready copy, and an indelible-ink pen on a printer's proof. There are several reasons why a lead pencil is never used: Lead marks are indistinct and will fade over time. Corrections can easily be overlooked. Lead-pencil corrections can also be erased. Make sure you have permanent proof of your work.

Be consistent, clear, and neat. Remember, these marks are your signature.

TABLE 6-1. PROOFREADER'S MARKS

Explanation	Mark in Margin	Mark in Copy	Corrected Copy
delete letter	ℓ	the careful /reader	the careful reader
delete word	ℓ	the ~~careful~~ reader	the reader
close up space	◡	the careful r͡eader	the careful reader
delete and close up space	ℓ	the careful r/eader	the careful reader
insert letter	a	the cᵣeful reader	the careful reader
insert word	careful	the ᵣreader	the careful reader
lowercase letter	(lc)	/The careful reader	the careful reader
lowercase letters	(lc)/(3)	/The /careful /Reader	the careful reader
lowercase word	(lc)	T̲H̲E̲ careful reader	the careful reader

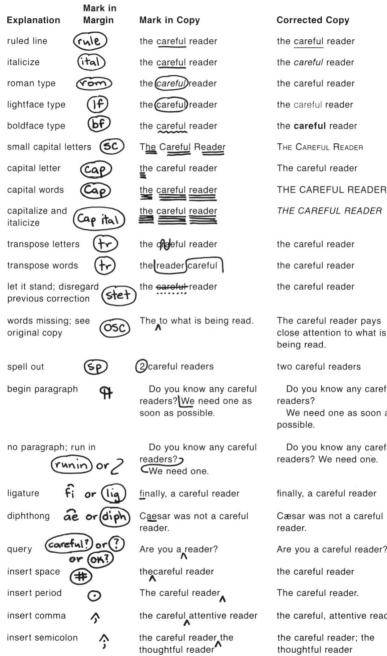

Explanation	Mark in Margin	Mark in Copy	Corrected Copy
ruled line	rule	the careful reader	the careful reader
italicize	ital	the careful reader	the *careful* reader
roman type	rom	the (careful) reader	the careful reader
lightface type	lf	the (careful) reader	the careful reader
boldface type	bf	the careful reader	the **careful** reader
small capital letters	sc	The Careful Reader	THE CAREFUL READER
capital letter	cap	the careful reader	The careful reader
capital words	Cap	the careful reader	THE CAREFUL READER
capitalize and italicize	Cap ital	the careful reader	*THE CAREFUL READER*
transpose letters	tr	the cafeful reader	the careful reader
transpose words	tr	the reader careful	the careful reader
let it stand; disregard previous correction	stet	the careful reader	the careful reader
words missing; see original copy	osc	The to what is being read.	The careful reader pays close attention to what is being read.
spell out	sp	2 careful readers	two careful readers
begin paragraph	¶	Do you know any careful readers? We need one as soon as possible.	Do you know any careful readers? We need one as soon as possible.
no paragraph; run in	runin or ⌐	Do you know any careful readers? We need one.	Do you know any careful readers? We need one.
ligature	fi or lig	finally, a careful reader	finally, a careful reader
diphthong	æ or diph	Caesar was not a careful reader.	Cæsar was not a careful reader.
query	careful? or ? or OK?	Are you a reader?	Are you a careful reader?
insert space	#	thecareful reader	the careful reader
insert period	⊙	The careful reader	The careful reader.
insert comma	⋏	the careful attentive reader	the careful, attentive reader
insert semicolon	⋏	the careful reader the thoughtful reader	the careful reader; the thoughtful reader

Explanation	Mark in Margin	Mark in Copy	Corrected Copy
insert colon	⊙	the careful reader∧	the careful reader:
insert apostrophe	⩔	the careful readeřs guide	the careful reader's guide
insert quotation marks	⩔ | ⩔	˅the careful reader˅	"the careful reader"
subscript	∧	H₂O	H_2O
superscript	⌄	the careful reade②r	the careful reader²
asterisk	✳	the careful˅reader	the careful* reader
dagger	† or (set dagger)	the careful reader∧	the careful reader†
double dagger	‡ or (set double dagger)	the careful reader∧	the careful reader‡
slash (virgule)	/ or (set slash)	the careful reader∧	the careful reader/
parentheses	(/)	the∧careful∧reader	the (careful) reader
brackets	⸦/⸧	the∧careful∧reader	the [careful] reader
invert	⊘	the careful reader (inverted)	the careful reader
indent 1 em	▯	⸧the careful reader	the careful reader
indent 2 ems	▣ or ⬜	⸧the careful reader	the careful reader
en dash	$\frac{1}{N}$	1948⏀1955	1948–1955
1-em dash	$\frac{1}{M}$	Reading carefully⏀not something everyone can do.	Reading carefully—not something everyone can do.
hyphen	=/=	Read word∧for∧word.	Read word-for-word.
straighten line	══	the careful reader	the careful reader
align	‖ or (align)	‖the careful reader	the careful reader
move down	⊔	the cᵃreful reader	the careful reader
move up	⊓	the cⁿreful reader	the careful reader
move left	⸦ or (fl)	⸦the careful reader	the careful reader
move right	⸧ or (fr)	the careful reader ⸧	the careful reader
open type	(open)	the careful reader	the careful reader
close type	(close) or (kern)	the carleful reader	the careful reader
fix hole	(bad rag)	Reading carefully is something not ⬭ everyone can do.	Reading carefully is something not everyone can do.

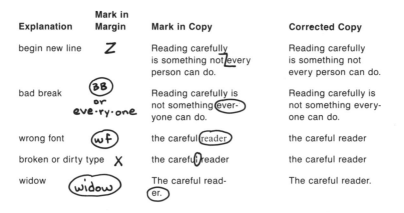

Explanation	Mark in Margin	Mark in Copy	Corrected Copy
begin new line	Z	Reading carefully is something not every person can do.	Reading carefully is something not every person can do.
bad break	ßß or eve·ry·one	Reading carefully is not something every- yone can do.	Reading carefully is not something every- one can do.
wrong font	wf	the careful reader	the careful reader
broken or dirty type	X	the careful reader	the careful reader
widow	widow	The careful read- er.	The careful reader.

WHERE THE MARKS GO

▶ The proofreader should indicate inside the copy—with a vertical | , slanted / , or horizontal line — ; a horizontal s-curve ∽ ; a circle ○ ; a half-circle ⌒ ; two half-circles ℃ ; a caret ∧ or ∨ , or a Z-mark Z , where the change is to be made.

▶ The instructive proof mark, the one indicating what the change is, is made in the margin.

▶ Every in-text mark must correspond to a marginal mark.

Some proofreaders yield to the temptation to omit the marginal mark and write instructions directly inside the copy. And there is sometimes good argument for doing so, especially if there is insufficient marginal space but ample leading between the letters, words, and lines of type. However, this is not recommended for a variety of reasons. An in-text correction, with no marginal mark, is much more likely to be missed than a marginal correction that instantly flags the line where the correction is to be made and what the correction should be. In-text instructions by the proofreader can also interfere with the editor's in-text marks, if there are any. So if you are tempted to make your instructions in the text, weigh the disadvantages first.

When instructions are made in the margin, use only one margin, not both, for each column of type. If there is more than one column of type on the page, proof marks for all columns should be systematically either on their left or their right—and not on the right margin for one and the left margin for another (unless there are only two columns of type on the page and the middle margin is narrow).

Because there may be more than one correction on a line, begin making proof marks at the far left side of the margin, separate each mark with a slant, and work toward the right. Make sure your instructions are positioned exactly parallel to the line being corrected.

Overcrowding sometimes occurs in one margin, and some proofreaders will make corrections in both margins, using whichever margin is closer to the error. The problems this creates outweigh any real justification for using this method. The corrections will not be in order, and jumping from one margin to another, then back to the text in search of the error, can often cause confusion for the typist or typesetter. Avoid this procedure if at all possible.

WHAT THE MARKS MEAN

The *circle* ◯ is used inside the text around a word that is to be reset in another font or face or around numbers that are to be spelled out. In the margin, circle the instruction. Don't circle words that are to be typed or typeset. Broken or dirty type is circled in the text, but the corresponding marginal mark, **X** , is not circled because it could be mistaken for the now-obsolete symbol for a period, Ⓧ . The circle is also used in the text to indicate a bad rag, which is a hole of space in the copy created by erratic line breaks. Make a circle inside the hole, then in the margin write (bad rag) or (hole) or (fix rag) (circled). To assist the typesetter in correcting a bad rag, see Margin Rag on page 116. Circle a bad word break, and in the margin write (BB) (circled) or write out the correct word break (don't circle).

The circle is used in-text for words that the proofreader may question for some reason. The marginal query mark, (?) should also be circled, or the typist or typesetter might set a question mark. Also circle in-text any unusual word that might be questioned by the typist or typesetter, and in the margin write (ok) or (sic) or (cq) (circled) to indicate the unusual but correct spelling. The period can be easily lost in the margin and should be circled: ⊙ So should the colon: (:) . The space symbol (#) should also be circled to avoid confusion with the symbol for pound or number (which is not circled).

The following marginal instructions should also be circled: (stet) for let it stand, (lc) for lowercase, (cap) for capitalize, (clc) for capitalize and lowercase, (sc) for small capital letters, (ital) for italicize, (rom) for roman type, (bf) for boldface type, (lf) for lightface type, (wf) for wrong font, (tr) for transpose, (sp) for spell it out, (fig) to set in figures or numbers, (fl) for flush left lines or margins, (fr) for flush right lines or margins, (run in) to delete paragraph indentations, (DNS) for do not set, (TK) for additional copy to come, (PE) for printer's error, and (AA) for author's alteration. In-text instructions for these marks follow.

The *dele* ℒ , pronounced dee-lee, is a marginal correction meaning to delete. It is rarely drawn properly and is often mistaken for an *e*. Practice drawing it correctly. The dele should not be used alone unless an empty space is intended or unless the result is obvious. Be cautious when using it alone, for what may look obvious to you, may not look that way to the typist or typesetter. For example, you want to give instructions to delete the hyphen in the word "by-pass." If you use the dele sign alone and if the instruction is followed precisely, the result is "by pass" when you may have intended "bypass." Deletion of a hyphen at the end of a line of type may also create the same kind of confusion unless additional instructions, such as a close-up sign, are given.

A *close-up sign* ○ should accompany the dele sign to indicate "bypass" ℒ . This sign is used to close up space between letters and words and is drawn both in the text and the margin. If it is drawn carelessly, the result may be the closing up of unintended characters or words. The sign is not used to close up tiny spaces between letters and words or to close up lines of type (see discussion on letter and word spacing on pages 105–108).

The *top part of the close-up sign* ⌢ is used in the text and in the margin to indicate a ligature, the joining of two letters (ff becomes ff). It is also used for the diphthong (ae becomes æ). The respective marginal marks for these are ⟨lig⟩ and ⟨diph⟩ , circled.

A *caret* ∧ in the text should be used to flag an insertion of a word and most punctuation marks. Draw the caret at the bottom of the line where the insertion is to be made. A corresponding caret ∧ is used in the margin to umbrella these marks: the comma ⟨,⟩ , the semi-colon ⟨;⟩ , and the subscript mark ⟨∧⟩ . A marginal caret over a letter, word, or numeral insertion is not necessary.

An *inverted caret* ∨ goes inside the text to indicate the following insertions, and again under the insertions in the margin: apostrophe ∨ , quotation marks ∨ ∨ , linear signs ∨ or ∨ , superscript mark ∨ , and the asterisk ❀ . Inside the text, draw the inverted caret at the top of the line where the insertion is to be made.

The *slant* or *virgule* / has many uses and is also a type character. It is used in the text to indicate lowercase. ¢APITAL or ¢APITAL becomes capital. C/APITAL or C/APITAL becomes Capital. Marginal marks are circled (lc) and (clc) (or (ulc) , for upper- and lowercase), respectively.

When there is more than one correction on a line of type, the slant is also used in the margin to separate each marginal instruction.

$$\wedge \; / \; \mathcal{L} \; / \; \text{(ital)}$$

If two identical changes occur consecutively on the same line of copy, it isn't necessary to repeat the change in the margin. Make the marginal instruction once, then follow with two slants instead of one. If more than three identical changes occur consecutively, make one slant, then follow with the number of times the change occurs. Circle the number.

②// Read pages /7 and /8.

(lc)/④ I went /Home, to /Town, to the /Bank, and back /Home.

If a slant is to be typed or typeset as part of the copy, place a caret in the text at the appropriate place; the marginal mark is a slant / (not circled), or write the words (set slant) (circled) in the margin.

A *vertical line* | through a letter inside the copy indicates a change or deletion; between two letters it can be used instead of a caret to indicate an insertion of a letter space or an additional letter(s). The vertical line must be accompanied by marginal instructions. Words or letters to be substituted or added in the text are written in the margin and are not circled. Remember, the marginal space mark is ⊕ (circled).

Two vertical lines in the margin ‖ indicate that a line of type should be vertically aligned with the other lines. ⊏ or ⊐ may also be used to indicate flush left or flush right lines or margins.

A *horizontal line* ── is drawn through an entire word if it is to be changed or deleted. If the word is to be exchanged for another word, write out the word in the margin, but don't circle it. The dele sign is not necessary. If a word is to be deleted entirely, the marginal mark is the dele sign. This is one instance where the dele sign is not accompanied by the close-up sign, as it would specify that you want it connected to the adjoining words.

One horizontal line is drawn directly under the word or words that you want italicized. The marginal instruction is ⒤tal , circled. If a rule (underscore) is intended, draw the horizontal line under the word(s), then write ⓡule or ⓤnderscore (circled) in the margin. For typeset copy, you must also indicate in the margin the weight of the rule (see discussion on rules, page 100).

A *wavy horizontal line* ∿∿∿ under a word instructs the typist or typesetter to make it boldface. The marginal mark is ⓑf (circled).

When a word must be boldface and italic, underscore with both a horizontal line and a wavy line, then write and circle ⓑf ital in the margin.

Two horizontal lines ═ under a letter or word indicate that small capital letters are needed. The marginal mark is ⓢc (circled). Three horizontal lines ≡ are used for capital letters, and the marginal mark is ⓒap (circled). And four horizontal lines ≣ are instructions for capital italicized letters or words. The marginal mark is (cap ital) (circled).

Two horizontal lines, one above and one below a word or line of type, ⚊ mean that horizontal alignment is needed.

A *bracket* in the text and in the margin are instructions to move the word or line up ⊓ or down ⊔ or left ⊏ or right ⊐ . A set of brackets facing away from each other ⊐⊏ are instructions to center the copy. If the brackets face each other ⊏⊐ , the copy will be justified.

A *paragraph symbol* ¶ is used as an in-text instruction to begin a new paragraph. If it isn't drawn carefully, it can be confused with the space symbol # . Another symbol used for a new paragraph is an L-shaped symbol ⌊ . Make corresponding symbols for marginal instructions and circle them. More common in typeset copy is the use of an open box in the margin ▢ , with a number inside to indicate the precise point measurement of the indentation. For example, ▢ is the symbol for a one-em space or indentation, ▣ for a two-em space or indent, and so on. ▨ is the symbol for a one-en space or indent.

A *curved line* ⌐ in-text is the instruction to run in one line of copy with another line, such as joining a sentence to a paragraph above it. Two shorter lines ⊂ᴐ may also be used symbolically to join the two. The marginal instruction is (run in) (circled).

Three checks ✓✓✓ or circled (eq. #) in the margin tells the typesetter that letters or words are unevenly spaced. A check mark at the letter space or word space in-text will indicate the places affected.

A *small vertical line* | can be used between those typeset letters or words where there is too much space. And a *plus sign* + in the text is used between the occasional word or letter to point out a tightness in spacing. Circled marginal instructions are (**kern**) and (**open**) , respectively. (See discussion on letter and word spacing on pages 105-108.) If all letters or words are too tight or too far apart in typeset copy, write and circle (**open type**) or (**close type**) at the top of the page. Make sure you have double-checked the instructions (type specifications) to the typesetter before making your decision. The odd spacing could be intentional. These instructions are not used in typed copy.

A *horizontal S-curve* ᴖ around letters or words inside the text is used to transpose them. The marginal instruction for transpose is the circled letters (**tr**) . If the copy type is so small that even two letters or words may be obscured by the ᴖ mark, circle them, then write (**tr**) (circled) in the margin. If the transposition is complicated or likely to be misunderstood, circle all of the affected words and write them out correctly in the margin. Sentences may be transposed by numbering them, in the text, in sequential order in which they should appear, then writing (**tr**) (circled) in the margin.

The word *stet* is Latin for *let it stand*. It is written and circled (**stet**) in the margin to void a previous proofreading correction or change. In the text, place dots under the letter(s) or word(s) affected.

Out, See Copy (**OSC**) is a marginal note that some words in the dead copy have been accidentally omitted from the live copy. A caret is used in the live copy text to mark the spot where the omission begins. So that the typist or typesetter will not have to search through the dead copy for the missing words, also mark the area in the dead copy with carets (where the omission begins and ends), then write (**OSC**) with a nonreproducing pen in the margin of the dead copy. Avoid using (**sc**) for "see copy," as this is the instruction for small capital letters. If only a word or a few words are missing from the live copy—and if there is enough room to write them in the margin—do so and spare the typist or typesetter the trouble of having to search through the dead copy.

The *invert sign* ℃ is used when a letter or word or line of type has been printed upside down. Unlikely to happen in computer typography, this can occur in handset metal typesetting or in a careless paste-up of typeset copy. Circle the affected character(s), then use the invert sign as a marginal mark.

Other symbols are used for letters or numbers that have similar shapes and could be misinterpreted by the typist or the typesetter:

O   for the letter o

∅   for the numeral 0

λ   for the numeral 2

Ƶ   for the letter z

1   for the numeral 1

7   for the numeral 7

ⓔⓛ   for the lowercase l

Sometimes there is no symbol or straightforward means to instruct the typesetter, especially for mathematical, scientific, or technical terms; reference marks such as the dagger or asterisk; the ampersand; bullet; and equal sign. Write out the instruction.

Don't invent new proof marks. They will confuse the person reading the corrections, and later even you may not recognize them or what they stand for.

Table 6-2 shows the original copy and Table 6-3 shows the proofreader's marks to correct the new copy.

TABLE 6-2. ORIGINAL (DEAD) COPY

Proofreading for Perfect Copy

Proofreading is a step-by-step procedure which must be followed carefully.

First you will compare the original (dead) copy against the newly typed or typeset (live) copy. You will either comparison read alone, with a copyholder, or with the aid of a tape recorder. After comparison reading, read the live copy again as many times as is necessary to find and correct all the errors. When there is no dead copy to compare the live copy against, you will read the live copy alone. This procedure is called noncomparison reading.

A proofreader is not only responsible for typographical and spelling errors, copy omissions, and format, but often for style, word usage, grammar, and punctuation as well. Some of these duties may require more editorial or academic training than some proofreaders may have, but you should give as much back-up support as you are qualified, and allowed, to do.

Read slowly. Read carefully. Research before you query. And remember, all corrections you make, or changes you suggest, must be approved by the writer or editor before they are typed.

The proofreader has additional duties if the copy is then typeset. The reader's proof, as this typeset copy is called, should be read for typographical errors and deviations from the original (dead) copy. These proofs are also read by the writer and the editor. Make sure that their changes—and your corrections—are combined on one proof before it is sent to the typesetter for revisions. When revisions are made, read the revised proof as thoroughly as you read the first proof. *New* errors can occur as the *old* ones are corrected, so **keep your eyes open!**

TABLE 6-3. NEW (LIVE) COPY WITH PROOFREADER'S MARKS

⊐⊏	⊐**Proofreading for Perfect Copy** ⊏
=/=	Proofreading is a step⌄by⌄step procedure which must be followed carefully.
③ | will	⊐First you⌄compare the original (dead) copy against the newly typed or typeset (live)
⊙	copy⌄You will either comparison read alone, with a copyholder, or with the aid of a tape recorder. After comparison reading, read the
ℓ	live copy again as many ~~many~~ times as is necessary to find and correct all the errors.
ℰ	When there is no d⌀ead copy to compare the live copy against, you will read the live
hole	copy alone. This procedure is called ⊂⊃ noncomparison reading.
(stet)	A proofreader is ~~not only~~ responsible for typographical and spelling errors, copy omissions and format, but often for style, word usage, grammar, and punctuation as well. Some of these duties may require
(lc) |③	more ⌿Editorial or ⌿Academic ⌿Training than some proofreaders may have, but you should give as much back-up support as you are qualified, and allowed, to do.
(tr) ⌒	|Read carefully.⌐Read slowly.⌐ Research be⌣fore you query.⌐
run in	⌐And remember, all corrections you make, or changes you suggest, must be approved by the writer or editor before they
¶	are typed.⌐The proofreader has additional duties if the copy is then typeset. The
⌄/⌃ ⌒	reader⌿s proof⌄as this typeset copy is called, should be read for typo⌣graphical errors and deviations from the original (dead) copy. These proofs are also read by the writer and
their | ⅟M	the editor. Make sure that ~~there~~ changes⊖
⅟M	and your corrections⊖are combined on one

(cont.)

TABLE 6-3. *(cont.)*

proof before it is sent to the typesetter for revisions. When revisions are made, read the revised proof as thoroughly as you read the first proof. *New* errors can occur as <u>old</u> ones are corrected, so keep your eyes op-en!

COPY EDITOR'S MARKS

The proofreader's and copy editor's marks are very similar. The major difference is how they are used. The proofreader's marks are both at the point of trouble in-text and in the margin. Copy editing instructions are in-text, and each mark is explicit and self-explanatory. Many of the copy editor's marks are simply a logical combination of what the proofreader uses both in-text and in the margin. In fact, editors who work with single-spaced copy may use the proofreader's method of in-text flags and marginal corrections, or sometimes a combination of both methods. If you know the proofreader's marks, you will have no trouble recognizing and understanding the copy editor's marks.

Editing is usually done before the copy is typed or keyed into the computer by the copy typist. The typist incorporates editorial changes while typing the original copy. As the copy editing marks are already inside the text, the typist doesn't have to interrupt typing speed to look in the margin for instructions. If the copy is already keyed and printed out before the editor makes changes, the editor will either use the proofreader's method to make changes or will make instructions in-text on the printout and place a check mark in the margin of the printout beside the lines where the changes were made. This copy will eventually become the dead copy that will be compared by the proofreader with the newly typed (live) copy.

7 WORKING WITH TYPE

Typefaces are a daily part of our lives, impossible to escape whether we are reading a book or a billboard, a recipe or a road map, movie credits or magazines. And identifying them is a fascinating adventure.

A conservative estimate of the number of typefaces in circulation is between 20,000 and 25,000. And the list is growing daily. These faces, each with distinctive characteristics, have one common purpose: to make thoughts visible.

An interest in typeface designs adds another dimension—and considerably more enjoyment—to the proofreader's job.

Expertise in type identification contributes even more to your professional worth. Every proofreader should at least know what makes one typeface different from another. For it will be your job, especially if you work for a typesetter or printer, to determine if it was set in the right face.

TYPE CLASSIFICATION

Because of the variety of typefaces, an established order has been attempted over the years. But type classification, as this arrangement has been called, has long been a source of debate among typographers, and no precisely systematic or universally accepted order exists. To further confuse the beginning student of type, some faces belong to several of these classifications. Below is one attempt at classification that groups the typefaces by stress (vertical or diagonal), thick and thin strokes, and serifs.

Serif (or Roman)

Letters have serifs (which are little cross-strokes at the ends of the main strokes) and varying contrast of thick and thin strokes.

Old Style.   Letters resemble Roman inscriptions, are wide, round, and open, with pointed serifs curving into the stroke, and gentle contrasts between light and heavy strokes.

ITC Garamond, Caslon 540,
Goudy Old Style

Transitional.   Letters are basically old style but show some adaptation to modern type. Serifs become more perpendicular, and thick and thin strokes become more defined.

Baskerville II, Times Roman, Century Schoolbook

Modern.   Letters are more mechanically perfect than old style and transitional, and their thick and thin strokes are more sharply designed. Serifs are straight, flat, and vertical or horizontal.

Bodoni, ITC Modern

Modern Serif

Because of their contemporary look, which contrasts so greatly with Roman type, some serif faces must be classified separately.

Square.   Letters are basically uniform in stroke with heavy slab serifs and no bracketing.

Clarendon, Lubalin Graph, Stymie

Round.   Letters employ the rounded shape of Roman type and the serifs are round and heavy.

Souvenir, Windsor

Inscribed. Letters are basically sans serif but the stems and bases widen slightly, giving a slightly chiseled effect, which suggests a serif.

Serif Gothic, ITC Korinna, ITC Friz Quadrata

Sans Serif

Letters have no serifs and very little contrast between thick and thin strokes. Also called Gothic in the United States.

Futura II, Triumvirate, Avant Garde Gothic

Script

Letters have no serifs and are designed to resemble handwriting.

Brush, Park Avenue, Commercial Script

Ornamental

Letters have fanciful designs and are used primarily to catch attention or evoke a mood.

Black Letter

Also called Old English, Gothic (in Europe), or text letters (not to be confused with text type). Letters resemble hand-drawn letters made by scribes. The vertical strokes and angles are heavy and broad, with delicate and ornamental hairlines.

Old English, ITC Zapf Chancery

TYPE CATEGORIES

For practical purposes, typefaces can be consolidated into two general categories, which cross all classifications of type.

Display Type

Most typefaces are display faces, an appropriate adjective, as they function primarily to establish a particular mood or emotion. They create attention. They are often the message, rather than the conveyor of one. Display type can be found in nearly all classifications of type. Designs range from stark, straight lines to fancy flourishes, with many variations in between. Uncomfortable to read for any length of time, display type is primarily used in headlines and brief messages, such as advertisements containing a few lines of copy, invitations, and announcements.

STENCIL, Windsor, Americana,

Univers, ITC Bauhaus,

ITC Benguiat,

ITC Eras Outline, Stymie

Text Type

Only a handful of typefaces of those thousands available are the ones we see and read most often. These text faces (also called book faces) are primarily from the Roman classification. Their shapes, strokes, and serifs are designed to link the letters into groups (words), allowing the eyes to flow smoothly from one letter to the next. A text face does not attract attention and is therefore easier to read. Text type is used for most books, magazine articles, dictionaries, and long body copy appearing in advertisements.

English Times
ITC Century

TYPE NAMES

The names of typefaces are copyrighted and owned by companies that have exclusive rights to their use. Their designs, however, are much more difficult to protect. And because of the wide public appeal of some typefaces, companies that do not own the original typeface often create a similar (but not identical) typeface to offer their customers. The resulting typefaces are copyrighted faces that may look like a well-known typeface to the untrained, but have slight variations *and* different names. Helvetica is a popular typeface that has many imitators:

Triumvirate
Helvetica

When a specific typeface isn't available, substituting another typeface with similar characteristics is common practice among some typesetters and printers and is generally accepted by their customers as well, who often don't know the difference. But a proofreader should be prepared to know what makes one typeface different from another. There will be many times during your proofreading career when you will be called upon to identify typefaces. You will need to know where to look and how to find them.

Typography classes or lectures are rare except in art design schools or through sponsorship by print professional organizations. Most proofreaders learn how to identify typefaces on the job or on their own. Learning the basics of type identification is not so hard to do. Use your typeface book. Start by comparing those typefaces you proofread most often with the corresponding faces in your typeface book. You will soon know the characteristics of those faces so well that you will be ready to tackle some new ones.

IDENTIFYING TYPE

Unless you are an expert, and few people are, the only way to identify a typeface is by comparing the elements of individual letters that have been typeset to those in a typeface book. The size, the shape, and the position of these elements is the key. (See Table 7-1.)

The Letters

Comparing individual letters is the way to begin. Start with the lowercase letter *g,* one of the most distinctive letters in the alphabet.

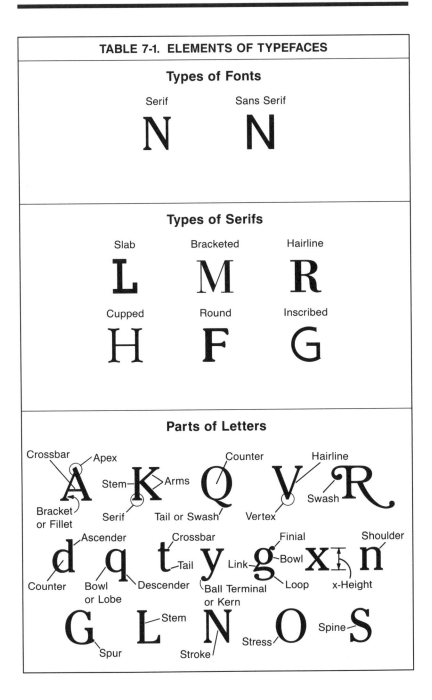

TABLE 7-1. ELEMENTS OF TYPEFACES

Palacio

abcdefghijklmnopqrstuvwxyz   g

ITC Korinna

abcdefghijklmnopqrstuvwxyz   g

Garamond

abcdefghijklmnopqrstuvwxyz   g

Artcraft

abcdefghijklmnopqrstuvwxyz   g

Goudy Old Style

abcdefghijklmnopqrstuvwxyz   g

Using the *g* as a preliminary guide to typeface identification can eliminate many false leads. The elements of the *g* are the bowl, the loop, the finial, and the link between the bowl and the loop.

Once you think the typeset *g* has been identified as a match with one in the typeface book, go on to a few other letters in the book. Compare capital letters *T, E, F, H, A,* as well as the lowercase letters *t, e, f.* The crossbars of these letters can be high, low, or centered, or long or short, and provide valuable clues to identification.

ITC Century

T, E, F, H, A   t, e, f

ITC Benguiat

T, E, F, H, A   t, e, f

The thickness of strokes in the capital letters *O, N, L* can also help you identify the specific face.

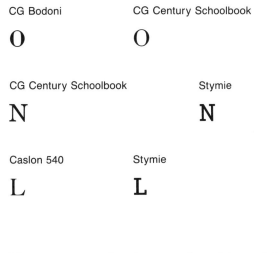

CG Bodoni

O

CG Century Schoolbook

O

CG Century Schoolbook

N

Stymie

N

Caslon 540

L

Stymie

L

Next, compare the shape and position of the capital *O*.

Stymie

O

CG Bodoni

O

Artcraft

O

Then, compare the height and shape of the bowls on the capital *R* or *P*.

Clarendon

R, P

Baskerville

R, P

Serif or Sans Serif

With their many different shapes, angles, and sizes, serifs (or the absence of them) give obvious identification clues.

Examine the difference between these typefaces:

Baskerville II (serif)
abcdefghijklmnopqrstuvwxyz
ABCDEFGHIJKLMNOPQRSTUVWXYZ
1234567890.,;:''&!?$

Bodoni (serif)
abcdefghijklmnopqrstuvwxyz
ABCDEFGHIJKLMNOPQRSTUVWXYZ
1234567890.,;:''&!?$

Triumvirate (sans serif)
abcdefghijklmnopqrstuvwxyz
ABCDEFGHIJKLMNOPQRSTUVWXYZ
1234567890.,;:''&!?$

Futura II (sans serif)
abcdefghijklmnopqrstuvwxyz
ABCDEFGHIJKLMNOPQRSTUVWXYZ
1234567890.,;:''&!?$

When you are using serifs as a guide to type identification, it is important to remember that a larger size or weight type is not always a photographic reproduction of its smaller counterparts. Serifs that look attractive in small type, but not so pleasing in a larger or bolder size, are sometimes modified or eliminated altogether by the designer. Always compare type in one size and weight to type of the same size and weight in the typeface book.

Stymie

y y *y* **y** **y** **y**

Serifs link one letter to the next, one word to the next. This type is easiest to read, especially in long copy.

While sans serif faces are unquestionably more legible than serif faces, they are not necessarily more readable. There are exceptions. Helvetica, as just one example, is sans serif. Its classic simplicity and perfect symmetry make this typeface as easy to read as a text (serif) face.

Modern typesetting equipment can magnify, reduce, expand, condense, or curve type. Distortion can result. Magnifying or expanding type will make the typeface appear heavier or bolder; it can also round out some of the edges of a typeface, such as finely chiseled serifs. For positive identification, it is important to know what composition process has occurred.

magnified, reduced,

expanded, condensed

The x-Height

Another aid to type identification is studying the x-height. All lowercase letters have an x-height, and many of them have ascenders and descenders that can also help you distinguish one typeface from another.

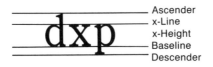

Ascender
x-Line
x-Height
Baseline
Descender

The x-height is the height of the body of the typeface. The ascender is the element rising above the x-height. The descender is the part dropping below the x-height.

Letters with ascenders: b d f h i k l t

Letters with only x-heights: a c e m n o r s u v w x z

Letters with descenders: g p q y j

The proportions of these elements vary among typefaces. The x-heights can be small or large; ascenders and descenders may be short or long.

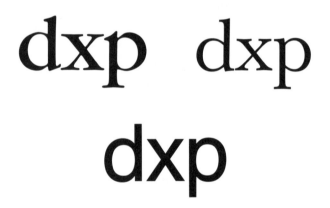

It is easy to confuse letters with similar shapes and characteristics, especially if you are not reading as slowly as you should. Let your eyes follow all contours of each letter as you read. Remember, the top half of letters is more recognizable than the lower half. Ascenders and descenders also help in quick letter recognition. Letters that are x-height are harder to recognize quickly.

Triumvirate

HANDBOOK FOR PROOFREADING

Century Schoolbook

Handbook for Proofreading

Rhythm

A typeface design can also convey a certain rhythm. The more familiar you are with the typeface, the more pronounced the rhythm becomes. Study the shapes of each letter. Practice drawing them. Look at the whole body of type and try to feel its movement.

ITC Garamond, Caslon 540, Lubalin Graph, Microstyle, Benguiat Gothic

DEFINITIONS OF THE ELEMENTS

Apex—the inverted v-shaped juncture of two stems, as in *A*.

Arm—the short stroke beginning at the stem and ending free.

Ascender—the part of the lowercase letters *b, d, f, h, k, l, t* that extends above the x-line.

Bar—the horizontal stroke in the *A, H, e, t,* and other similar letters.

Bowl—a curved stroke fully enclosing a counter.

Counter—the fully or partially enclosed space within a letter.

Crossbar—the stroke cutting across a stem, as in *f, t.*

Descender—the part of the letters *g, j, p, q, y* that extends below the baseline.

Finial—the small stroke projecting from the top of the *g.* Also called an ear. Any nonserif ending of a stroke.

Link—the stroke connecting the top and bottom of the *g.*

Loop—the bottom part of the *g.*

Main Stem—the thicker stem of a letter, if one.

Serif—a line crossing (at the top and bottom) the strokes of a letter.

Spine—the main curved stroke of an *S* or *s.*

Stem—any vertical straight stroke (or main oblique straight stroke if the letter has no vertical stroke).

Stress—the thickening in a curved stroke.

Stroke—any straight or curved line that is necessary to form a letter.

Swash—a fancy flourish that replaces a terminal or serif.

Tail—the downward short stroke on *Q.*

Terminal—the finishing stroke on a letter not ending with a serif or finial.

Vertex—the v-shaped juncture of two stems, as in *V.*

x-Height—the height of lowercase letters, excluding ascenders and descenders.

8 | UNDERSTANDING THE PRINTER'S LANGUAGE

Instructions to typesetters, called type specifications (specs) or markup, are written in a technical but very simple language. They are, as proof marks are, a universal shorthand code that everyone connected with typesetting and printing must know— and most certainly the proofreader, who must determine whether the instructions were followed.

There are three primary pieces of information that the typesetter must have:

▶ type font   ▶ copy depth/line length/margins

▶ leading

These specifications are commonly written as a formula:

Goudy bf ital 10/11 [x 14]

This paragraph is set in Goudy (the name of the typeface) bold (the weight) italic (the posture). The typeface size is 10 points, the leading is 1 point (10-point type size plus 1-point leading equals 11 points total line height), the [is a flush left instruction, the] is a flush right instruction (therefore, the copy is justified), and × 14 is a 14-pica line length. These specifications will be explained in the following pages.

There are secondary instructions to the typesetter, as well, and they also will be explained.

TYPE FONT

Type font is a complete set of characters in one *typeface*, one *style*, and one *size*. It contains all uppercase and lowercase letters and includes punctuation marks, numerals, ligatures, and other special characters. To make sure that the proper type font has been set, match it to the corresponding one in the typeface book.

Face

This is the design of the type, and it will be specified to the typesetter by its copyrighted name. Helvetica and Goudy are examples of copyrighted names.

Style

The weight, width, and posture of a typeface are the style of the typeface. Each is independent of the other.

Weight is determined by the thickness of strokes. A typeface can have many weights: extra light, light, book, medium, demi-bold, semibold, bold, extra bold, ultra bold. Descriptive names and the degree of thickness can vary by typeface. A typeface book is your guide. The specified weight of the typeset copy should be an exact match to the corresponding weight in the book. When weight is not included in the type specifications, book or medium weight will be typeset.

Triumvirate Light

Type set in lightface often fades into the background, making reading difficult.

Triumvirate Medium

Type set in medium face weight is easier to read. Especially with small type, medium weight is more distinct than light or bold weights.

Triumvirate Bold

Boldface type is difficult to read. The density eliminates some of the white space inside and around the letters.

All typefaces have weight. Type of any size can be any weight. Small type can be bold or light or any weight in between. So can large type.

Width is the amount of horizontal space each letter covers. A typeface can have many widths: condensed, thin, extended, fat, book, extracondensed, elongated, compressed, expanded, or wide. As with weights, specific names and degrees of width can vary with each typeface. When width is not included in the type specifications, book width will be typeset. The letters in this paragraph are set in book width.

This typeface is condensed. As the letters are squeezed together, a single letter could easily be overlooked.

This expanded typeface should be proofread letter by letter. It is as difficult to read as large headline type.

All typefaces have width. Type of any size can be any width. Small type can be expanded or compressed. So can large type.

Posture   is the slant of the typeface. Display and script faces often have unique slants that are not labeled. Many text faces have fonts that slant to the right (italic). And computerized type can now slant faces to the left (back slant). The upright posture of a text typeface is called roman. Don't confuse this with the Roman type classification. When posture is not included in the type specifications, roman posture will be typeset. The letters in this paragraph are set in roman posture.

Italic typefaces are harder to read than roman faces.

Back slant typefaces are also harder to read than roman faces.

All typefaces have posture. Type of any size can be any posture.

The word *regular* has been omitted as a description of a typeface weight, width, or posture. A common but ambiguous term, it is often used by those seeking a type style that looks most "normal." As different typefaces may look regular or normal in a variety of ways, a more precise specification is essential. What's more, neither the typesetter nor the proofreader can be expected to do their job well with such vague instructions. Unless there actually exists a *regular* style for the particular type-face being set, those who typeset and proofread the type should ask for a more definite specification.

Size

The third characteristic of a typeface is probably its least under-stood dimension. It is important to remember that two different typefaces of the same size may not look—or actually measure— the same. That is why comparing type against one of the same face and size in a typeface book is the most accurate way to measure.

Many typeface books do not contain all faces and sizes of type, however, which is why the point gauge is the most conven-ient and common method of measuring. But it's an inexact sci-ence and has become even more so with the advent of computerized typesetting and photographic equipment. Even to the observant and practiced eye, it is an approximate measure, and those proofreaders who insist on absolutes may not easily understand it.

Points and Picas. Typefaces and other typographical ele-ments such as rules, bullets, hyphens, and dashes are measured in *points*, a system used by typesetters in America. There are several different units of measure in Europe and other parts of the world, one being the metric measure which, until recently, has met with resistance in the United States.

There are 72 points to an inch, approximately. Actually, a point is .0138 or about $1/72$ of an inch, but unless you are the typesetter or printer, you won't have the challenge of working with fractions.

Spaces created by type (leading, indentations, line length, copy depth) are measured in *picas*. Pica measurement is simply an extension of the point measure. As the measure in the point system gets larger, the measuring units change from points to picas, just as when the inch measure gets larger, its measuring unit changes from inches to feet.

There are 12 points to a pica, 6 picas to an inch. It is with this larger unit that space is measured.

Points and Picas

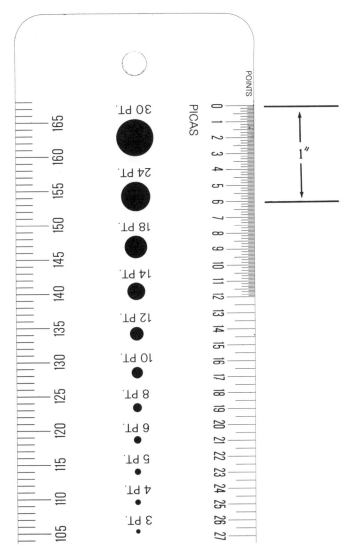

To measure type size and space, the proofreader will need the same tool the artist, typesetter, and printer use: a metal or transparent ruler (also called a line gauge), calibrated in points and picas. These measures are also available on a plastic sheet, usually 8½" by 11", called a transparency.

Most typefaces are designed in sizes and half-sizes from 4 to 144 points. Type measuring from 4 to 7 points is often seen in footnotes, ingredient labels, classified advertisements, or sometimes on a contract. A magnifying glass for proofreading this *mouse type* is recommended.

mouse type
mouse type
mouse type
mouse type

Type sizes that allow for more comfortable reading, such as in book texts, newspaper or magazine articles, and advertisements, are within the 9- to 14-point range, depending on the size characteristics of a particular typeface. Type this size is commonly referred to as *body type.*

body type   body type
body type   body type
body type   body type

Larger type sizes, sometimes called *display type*, range from 18 to 72 points. A 72-point typeface measures about one inch tall.

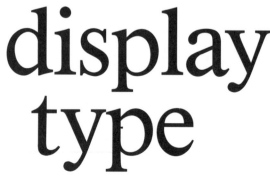

display type

Although typefaces can range up to 144 points in size, most computerized typesetting equipment doesn't print typefaces larger than 72 points for two reasons: (1) larger sizes are not generally provided in the computer program, and (2) the paper normally used to print out type isn't wide enough to contain much copy that size. Type larger than 72 points is usually set, letter by letter, on film by a special machine that is called a Typositor® [5].

Proofreading mistakes often occur with large type (15 points or larger). The eye cannot embrace the entire word. Proofreading large type should be done letter by letter.

What To Measure.   The rectangular block of metal used in offset printing is, for measuring purposes, the same as the type image produced by computer or photographic typesetting. It is the body and face on either that are important to those who must measure the type. The entire surface of the block is called the *body*, and the printing surface is the *face*. It is the body, not just the face, that is measured for size.

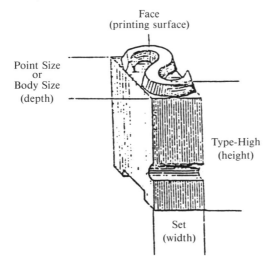

Face
(printing surface)

Point Size
or
Body Size
(depth)

Type-High
(height)

Set
(width)

---

[5] Photo Typositor is a photo-display unit manufactured by the Visual Graphics Corporation.

Most typeface ascenders and descenders fill—or at least come close to filling—the vertical space of the body, and the approximate size can be measured.

Some typefaces may look larger or smaller, depending on the proportions of their ascenders and descenders or x-heights. And as the face plus the space, if any, compose the body, this vertical dimension can sometimes present a problem for the beginner.

The face, not the actual measure, conveys the visual impression of size. But it is the body that produces the actual type measurement. A 10-point body produces a 10-point type; an 11-point body, an 11-point type; and so on.

The following typefaces are the same size.

Garamond

b g f y a c e m

Baskerville II

b g f y a c e m

Bodoni

b g f y a c e m

Century Book

b g f y a c e m

Triumvirate

b g f y a c e m

Using the Point Gauge. Even with a point gauge, type cannot be measured for accurate size, although the proofreader can get an approximate measure. Here's how:

Measuring from Ascender to Descender. Ascenders and descenders of many typefaces (and the proofreader must be experienced enough to know which typefaces) *almost* fill the body of a block of type. Find a word that contains both an ascender and a descender. By placing the point gauge at the 0 mark at the tip of the ascender, then measuring to the bottom tip of the descender, an approximate measure can be determined. A capital letter, if it is the height of the ascenders in that typeface, can be used instead of the ascender to measure.

ITC Century 42 pt.

Measuring by Line Height. Line height is the size of the type plus the amount of leading (spacing between the lines). If the leading is known, the type size can be determined by placing the point gauge at the 0 mark of the base of one line and measuring to the base of the following line. Subtract the points of lead. The number of points remaining is the type size. Leading measurement is further explained on page 102.

Using the Pica Gauge. In the following paragraph, select at least four lines of typeset copy to measure, including the leading (as it must be known to measure the type).

> The type in this paragraph is 10 points, leading 3 points, or 10/ 13. With the pica gauge, measure from the base of the first line to the base of the third line below it. These three lines measure three picas plus halfway between the 3-pica mark and the next half-pica mark. Total depth is 3 picas plus 3 points, which equals 39 points. Dividing by three equals 13 points. By subtracting 3 points of leading between each line of type, the remaining picas equal 30 points.

Three lines of any even-numbered point type measure exactly on the pica or half-pica mark. For example, three lines of 8-point type measure 2 picas; three lines of 10-point type equal 2¹/₂ picas. An odd number of points will strike halfway between the marks.

Using the Transparency. The plastic transparency shows points and other printing measurements, including one that measures a capital letter or, on some transparencies, a lowercase letter.

The letters on the transparency do not measure a true point size. They only measure a standard-size capital letter for standard-size typefaces. For example, a 12L letter on the following transparency illustration will closely match the size of a capital serif letter on a 12-point typeface. Lowercase letters on the transparency are for measuring standard-size lowercase letters.

Some transparencies will show letters with serifs; others will have letters with no serifs. It is best to measure serif type on transparencies with serif letters, sans serif type on transparencies with sans serif letters.

When matching type against capital or lowercase letters on a transparency, the proofreader must know whether the particular typeface being measured is of average size or whether it is one of those typefaces that is designed small. If it is one of the smaller designed typefaces, the letters on the transparency cannot be used to measure it. Go to your typeface book for comparison. If you are unsure about the type design or the actual size, ask fellow workers who are more familiar with type. A little study and practice, and you will soon know as much as they do.

Lines, dots, and other shapes of type, used to call attention to particular passages of copy, are not automatic measures either. Size and weight are determined by the artist. Specifications are written as point measurements in the margin beside the copy

PICAS   INCHES

HELVETICA REGULAR

E	4½	hmy
E	5	hmy
E	6	hmy
E	7	hmy
E	8	hmy
E	9	hmy
E	10	hmy
E	11	hmy
E	12	hmy
E	14	hmy
E	16	hmy
E	18	hmy
E	20	hmy
E	24	hmy
E	30	hmy

TIMES ROMAN

E	4½	hmy
E	5	hmy
E	6	hmy
E	7	hmy
E	8	hmy
E	9	hmy
E	10	hmy
E	11	hmy
E	12	hmy
E	14	hmy
E	16	hmy
E	18	hmy
E	20	hmy
E	24	hmy
E	30	hmy

where the lines or shapes are to appear. The proofreader will match these rules, bullets, stars, or squares to corresponding ones on the transparency.

A rule may be a $^1/_2$-point hairline rule ⎯⎯, a 1-point rule ⎯⎯, a 2-point rule ⎯⎯, and so on. The more points specified, the heavier and thicker the rule. Bullets, stars, and squares are also measured in points. They become larger as the point size increases (1-point bullet ·, 2-point bullet •). The most precise way that a proofreader has to measure these shapes is against a transparent gauge that contains ruled lines, bullets, or stars in a variety of sizes.

Wrong Font

If any of the elements in a type font has been set wrong, it has been set in the wrong font.

Face: If Helvetica type was specified but the copy was set in Goudy, it is in the wrong font.

Weight: If Helvetica bold was specified but the copy was set in Helvetica light, it is in the wrong font.

Width: If Helvetica condensed was specified but the copy was set in Helvetica extended, it is in the wrong font.

Posture: If Helvetica italic was specified but the copy was set in Helvetica regular, it is in the wrong font.

Size: If 10-point Helvetica was specified but the copy was set in 12-point Helvetica, it is in the wrong font.

The proofreader may circle the mistake in the copy and use the marginal instruction, a circled ⓦⓕ . It would be more helpful to the typesetter, however, if you circled the mistake in the copy and wrote out specific instructions, such as set Goudy bold   or   set Goudy 10 pt.   .

This keeps the typesetter from having to search back through the type specs for the information.

LEADING

The space around the type is equally important in design. It provides the frame for the typeface. If it is too tight, it can squeeze the type and make it dark and unreadable. If there is too much space, the type can float, causing a disruptive reading pattern.

Leading (rhymes with sledding), also called line spacing, is the second primary piece of information a typesetter must have to set type. This is the space, measured in points, between the lines of type both in the headline and in the body copy. Leading also refers to spacing between words and letters (word spacing and letter spacing), which will be explained later in this chapter.

Line Spacing

There is no rule dictating the proportion of leading to type size. It is an artistic decision, determined primarily by the typeface design, its size and style, x-height, ascenders, and descenders.

1. This paragraph is set in 10-point type with no leading. It is written as 10/10 . The first 10 indicates the size of type. The following 10 is the line height, the size of the type plus the amount of leading. When the line height is the same measure as the type size, it means that there is no leading, that the type is *set solid*. In most solid-type copy, the descender letters on one line will almost touch the ascender letters on the line below it. There will be exceptions in solid type where ascenders and descenders are not close to each other, or where they may even overlap, depending on the typeface design. This is a good reason always to measure the leading, even if you think you may know what it is just by looking at it.

2. This paragraph is set in 10-point type with 1-point leading. It is written in the formula as 10/11 . The 10 indicates the size of type. The 11 is the line height.

3. This paragraph is set in 10-point type with 2-point leading. It is written in the formula as 10/12 . The 10 indicates the size of type. The 12 is the line height.

How Leading Is Determined.   Some faces have big x-heights or long ascenders and descenders that will naturally call for more space between lines for attractive layout and comfortable reading. When there is not enough spacing between the lines of type, an often unattractive "bumping" will occur, as a descender on one line hits an ascender on the next line. If you don't know whether this bumping was intended by the artist or accidental because of a miscalculation, you should circle the affected letters and write and circle in the margin bumps.

These two lines of type illustrate
"bumping" ascenders and descenders.

Typefaces with small x-heights or short ascenders and descenders need less space between the lines, sometimes even minus line spacing. This is a reduction of space between lines of type to less than the point size of the typeface. For example, a 12-point typeface with a line height of $11^1/_2$ points is minus $^1/_2$ point of line spacing. Minus line spacing is very common in headline type and is also occasionally used with body type for special artistic reasons.

When upper- and lowercase letters are used with numerals (such as in a name and address), an uneven "color" is often created because of the size difference between the numerals and the lowercase letters. A more even distribution of space will occur by adding extra lead between the lines. The proofreader may offer this suggestion, but it will normally be a decision made by the artist.

The Colony Bank
9870 Third Avenue
Central City, Idaho 60800

The Colony Bank
9870 Third Avenue
Central City, Idaho 60800

Line length is another element of consideration for good leading. The longer the lines, the more spacing between them is needed to read smoothly and easily to the next line.

Additional leading is sometimes desired as a break between paragraphs. The instruction is not written in the standard formula shown at the beginning of the chapter. Instead, it is written in the margin beside the place in the copy where the extra leading is to appear. If the line height in a paragraph is 10 points, and an extra 4 points of leading is needed between paragraphs (making the line height 14 points between paragraphs), the artist will designate it by writing **+4** between the paragraphs that need the extra space. It normally will not be circled.

The leading between paragraphs 1 and 2 page 101 has an additional 4 points of space. Compare the difference with other paragraphs in this book.

Using the Point Gauge.

To determine if the leading is correct, type size must be known. Measure the typeface in paragraph 1 (page 101). It is 10 points. Next, place the point gauge at the 0 mark on the top of the x-height on a line. Follow the gauge down to the top of the x-height on the line below. (You may also place the point gauge at the 0 mark on the bottom of the x-height on a line and follow the gauge down to the bottom of the x-height on the line below.) The measure should be 10 points. Therefore, the type is 10 points solid (10/10). Type specifications with the number sequence 10/11 (measure paragraph 2 on page 101) would mean that the type size is 10 points with 1 point of leading; 10/12 (measure paragraph 3 on page 102) would mean 2 points of leading, and so on. To measure the extra leading between paragraphs 1 and 2, place the point gauge at the 0 mark on the top (or bottom) of the x-height on the last line of paragraph 1. Follow the gauge down to the top (or bottom) of the x-height on the first line of paragraph 2. It should measure 14 points, meaning there are 4 extra points of leading between the two paragraphs.

Using the Transparency. Transparencies contain another measuring gauge, a series of lines, by which leading can be determined. Use only the boxed lines for 10-point leading on your gauge. Go to paragraph 1. Place the top line of the box on the top of the x-height in the first line of copy. The remaining 10-point lines should fall at the same point on the x-height of the lines that follow. If they don't, and assuming the type size is correct, at least one of the leading measures is wrong.

Wrong Leading. If you are correcting a leading problem, you will mark the point of trouble, then in the margin write and circle one of the following: ⟨ld⟩ (add lead), ⟨⅋ld⟩ (delete lead), ⟨wr ld⟩ (wrong lead), ⟨eq ld⟩ (equalize lead). Or you may be more specific by giving the precise leading adjustment that is needed (⟨+1 pt. ld⟩ or ⟨−1 pt. ld⟩).

The space between lines one and two contains one point of lead. The lines below are set solid.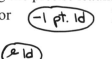

When it is not the entire line of type, but only a word or two that are improperly aligned, draw one horizontal line above the word (or words) and another line below. In the margin, make two horizontal lines in the margin, or write out in the margin and circle ⟨align⟩ . See Table 6-1.

This sentence is improperly aligned.

Word Spacing

Spacing between *typewritten* words is set in mechanical spacing units. Each word is a uniform distance from the next. It cannot be adjusted in any way.

The space between *phototypeset* words, also called a unit, is specified in the computer program to begin at a precise (but not mechanical) distance from each word. The amount of space that will fall between each word is calculated according to the characteristics of a particular typeface design and size. But unlike on typed copy, spacing adjustments between words can be made by the typesetter. Even when the spacing problem affects just a few words, the typesetter can adjust the spacing to open the tight spots or close up space.

As there are no instruments for the proofreader to measure word spacing units, you will be guided by the optical spacing effect. Between the affected words, use the ✛ sign to open space, the | sign to kern (close space). Marginal instructions are (open) and (close) , respectively.

This is not a job for the beginning proofreader or for anyone else who is not accustomed to working with typeset copy. Ideally, you will receive guidance from an expert for a few weeks, and you will soon develop good judgment and a fine eye for spacing problems. It is your job to help the typesetter through these tight, and sometimes loose, spots.

Bad Word Spacing. There is the likelihood of irregular word spacing in all typeset copy but most particularly in very large or very small or in all-capitalized type.

Where the spacing is too tight, words will run together.

If it is too far apart, the spaces create gaps that the eye must jump over to read.

Sometimes spacing problems will affect only a word or two in a sentence.

Copy with justified columns usually has word spacing irregularities. There is no easy solution. The copy is restricted to the narrow confines of equal-length lines. So that the copy will fit exactly on both margins, word spacing most likely will be uneven despite special custom-fitting by the typesetter.

When several consecutive lines of type are set with wide word spacing (to accommodate a justified margin), this can compound the spacing problem with "rivers" of white space that overpower the horizontal flow of type. The only solution is to add extra words to fill in the gaps.

Consecutive word breaks at the end of a line of justified type are still another problem and one which is often ignored, mainly because fixing a word break on one line often causes a new word break on the following line. But unless you have been instructed to ignore legitimate word breaks, you should circle all consecutive breaks.

Some spacing adjustments can be made by the typesetter, but unless the line length is increased or the copy is rewritten to the exact measure of the line, there is no happy solution. Working with justified copy is often the proofreader's (and the typesetter's) most frustrating and difficult chore.

The proofreader should look for word spacing problems in all typeset copy. Bad spacing is unattractive, hard to read, and can destroy an otherwise artistic and creative endeavor.

Letter Spacing

Also part of the leading process, letter spacing varies according to the size and design of the typeface and is automatically programmed into the computer or typesetting program. But spacing problems between occasional letters can and do occur. The proofreader judges good letter spacing not with the printer's tools but how it looks on paper. As with word spacing, it is an optical measurement, not a mathematical one. Each letter, and the space surrounding it, then the entire word or line of words, must be judged. It requires careful observation and practiced judgment to spot when one letter is too close to or too far from the next one.

Mechanically Spaced

READING

Optically Spaced

READING

Bad Letter Spacing.   The most likely candidates for irregular letter spacing problems are very small or large, headline-size type, display type, and all-capitalized letters.

An unfortunate choice of typeface can also create an insurmountable problem with certain combinations of letters:

Caslon No. 3

LAWYER

The only solution is to change the wording or the typeface.

Sometimes, though, type that is set far apart or close together is intended. *Positive* spacing is often used to set apart all-capital letters and words. *Negative* spacing, where letters or words touch, even overlap, can also be deliberate. Both are used as attention-getting devices, primarily in advertising. As both are hard to read, they normally are not used in long copy.

Goudy Old Style

ACADEMIC

ITC Lubalin Graph

Locomotion

If the artist wants unusual spacing between letters, it must be expressed precisely to the typesetter. Regular spacing (that which is already written in the program) does not require special instructions. To correct tight or wide spacing between letters, the proofreader uses the same marks and instructions as for word spacing.

Em and En Spacing

Paragraph Indentations. The blank spaces used before the beginning of a paragraph are called *em space* or *em quad*. The em, so called because the capital letter *M* is as wide as it is high, is a square of space as wide and as high as the size of type being set.

> This paragraph has a 1-em indentation. A 1-em indentation on 10-point type is space that is 10 points wide and 10 points high. A 1-em indentation on a line containing 6-point type is space that is 6 points wide and 6 points high. A 1-em indentation is most often used for copy with short lines. Long lines of copy require more. It is an artistic decision.

Sometimes an artist will specify indentations in picas instead of ems. It is not the usual way to specify indentations, but it can be, and is, done. The proofreader should make sure that the artist intended picas, especially if the indentation seems wider than it should normally be. Don't confuse the em and the pica when measuring.

> *En space* is one-half the width of an em, measuring about as wide as the capital letter *N*. A 1-en paragraph indentation on 10-point type is 5 points wide and 10 points high. This paragraph has a 1-en indentation.

Dashes. Em quads and en quads, also called muttons and nuts, have still another use as measures for short, ruled lines, or dashes.

There are four kinds of dashes that must be measured: the en dash, the em dash, the 2-em dash, and the 3-em dash. An en dash is half the width of an em dash. The 2-em dash is twice the width of an em dash, and the 3-em dash is three times as wide. A hyphen, which is also a dash, is an automatic measure in typesetting and its width will be determined by the typeface design and size.

On typewritten copy, the hyphen is indicated by one horizontal line between letters or words (-). The em dash is indicated by two typed horizontal lines (--). It should be circled and a precise measurement given to the typesetter. As there is no typewriter element that can indicate an en dash, a 2-em dash, or a 3-em dash, two horizontal lines are also used for each. The artist must circle the lines and specify the size dash in the margin.

Hyphens. Hyphens are used between word divisions at the end of a line. Other uses are to express a unit, such as with simple compound adjectives, nouns, or numbers; as suspension in a series; with some prefixes; or to avoid ambiguity:

chocolate-covered nut   decision-maker

twenty-three   ex-employee

2- and 3-hour sessions   re-sign the contract

Hyphens are designed to be centered on the x-height. And when used in lowercase letters, the position is usually ideal. When a hyphen is used with capital letters, it sometimes appears too low. Watch for this and ask the typesetter to raise it to an optically centered position. (Parentheses and brackets are also designed for lowercase letters and should be raised to line up with capital letters.)

En Dash.   The en dash is used between page numbers, dates or periods of time, and references:

pp. 551–558

during the period 1860–1865

chapters 1–3

The en dash should not be used to designate "from...to" or "between...and."

Use an en dash between compound adjectives and to separate hyphenated words:

pre–Space Age technology

high-temperature–low-temperature averages

The Chicago Herald–Tribune

Em Dash.   The em dash marks a sudden break in thought or tone; sets off (for clarity or emphasis) an added explanation or parenthetical element; separates an introductory series and the main part of the sentence; or introduces a name after a quotation:

> I was scared—but who wouldn't have been?

> The gloves—the hat, too—were leather.

> The book, the pen, the paper—all were on my desk.

> "...and a touch of grammar for picturesqueness."
> —Mark Twain

2-Em Dash.   A 2-em dash substitutes for missing letters.

> Robert J—— is the culprit.

3-Em Dash.   A 3-em dash indicates a missing word.

> I went to Lake ——— to sail my boat.

A 3-em dash is also used in bibliographies when the author of a work is the same as the author of the work that immediately precedes it.

> Ogilvy, David. *Confessions of an Advertising Man*, New York: Atheneum, 1963.
> ———. *Ogilvy On Advertising*, New York: Crown Publishers, Inc., 1983.

Always watch for incorrect usage of these dashes.

COPY DEPTH, LINE LENGTH, MARGINS

Copy depth, line length, and margins are the final instructions to the typesetter. Copy depth is usually not written into the formula for the following reasons. Line length and margins are part of the formula.

Copy Depth

Usually referring only to the body copy depth and not including the headlines, copy depth is how long the copy measures, in picas, from the first line through the last, including leading and any other spacing that may have been specified. A vertical measure may be given to the typesetter. It will be written beside the formula like this: 22 picas deep   . Or the depth may only be implied if a layout accompanies the type. The proofreader must check depth accordingly. For example, the depth for this page is 42^1/$_2$ picas.

The exact space in which the copy will fit is determined before the type is set, by a procedure called copyfitting. The artist calculates the area required for a given amount of typed copy in a specified typeface by a simple mathematical formula. If copyfitting is not done beforehand, the outcome may not be a very happy one. Miscalculation can cause the copy to run short of the planned copy depth. Or it could run too long. And either can ruin a creative concept.

Even when copyfitting has occurred, a rough layout (but in exact measurements) often accompanies the typed copy to the typesetter. This layout may (or may not) give the typesetter an alternative to overcome spacing problems, if there are any. If there is a mutual understanding between the artist and the typesetter, copy that runs too short may be set ^{1}/$_2$ point larger or if it runs too long it may be set ^{1}/$_2$ point smaller to fit the space in the layout. But most artists do not rely on this haphazard method of fitting copy to space.

Line Length

The way to measure the horizontal length of the lines of typeset copy will depend on the margins. As all lines in justified copy measure the same, the length is the number of picas it takes to fill any one line. In a rag margin where the line beginnings or endings vary in length, the longest line should be measured. This line cannot exceed the specified line length, although some of the other lines will be shorter.

The pica measure for line length on the copy specifications formula is always preceded by an $\times$. Instructions for a 14-pica line length will look like this: $\times$ 14 .

There are several artistic considerations that determine the line length: typeface design, the type size, leading, the amount of copy to be typeset, and the amount of space the artist has to work with. Generally, the larger the size type, the longer the line. A normal line of copy has between 55 and 60 characters or 9 to 10 words.

Lines that are exceedingly long or short are hardest to read. When a line of type is too long, the eyes tire before reaching the end. In addition, the eyes must then jump a longer distance back to the following line.

Short lines interrupt sentence structure. They also create more word breaks. When the eyes must continuously jump from one short line down to the next short line, it causes reader fatigue.

Margins

Column margins are the vertical patterns created by the lines of type. Instructions must be given for both the right and left margins. Following is a variety of margins from which the artist selects.

Flush Left. All left lines begin at the same vertical point on the left margin, except paragraph indentations, if indicated. If they are not indicated, the first lines of each paragraph are also flush left. Copy spec marks in the formula are either (fl) or ⌐ .

Flush Right. All right lines end at the same point on the right margin. Spec marks in the formula are either ⓕⓡ or ⅃ .

Ragged Left or Right. The left or the right margin has no specified minimum stopping point. There is always a maximum stopping point or line length. The typesetter ends the line where it looks appropriate within that specified line length, usually alternating a short line, then a longer line, followed by a shorter line, making a smooth, rhythmic pattern. (See Margin Rag on page 116.) A ragged margin usually assures even letter and word spacing. Spec marks are rl or rr , or } for either rag margin.

Each column of type has two margins. So where there is a flush or rag left margin, obviously there must be a flush or rag right margin. And instructions for both must be specified. For flush left/rag right: fl/rr or ⊏{ . This paragraph is set flush left/rag right.

Each column of type has two margins. So where there is a flush or rag left margin, obviously there must be a flush or rag right margin. And instructions for both must be specified. For rag left/flush right: rl/fr or {⅃ . This paragraph is set rag left/flush right.

Justified. With justified copy, both margins line up vertically except where paragraph indentations are indicated. When none is indicated, the first line in every paragraph is flush left, creating the need for extra leading between paragraphs as a break. Spec marks for justified copy are fl/fr (rarely used) or the word ⓙⓤⓢⓣⓘⓕⓨ or ⊏⅃ . The columns in this book have justified margins.

As mentioned in Word Spacing on page 105, the amount of space between the words, and letters, may be erratic because the lines will be vertically even. The proofreader should watch for very obviously irregular word or letter spacing. Sometimes it can be corrected; other times it cannot without cutting or adding copy. Word breaks also occur more often in justified copy than in copy with a rag margin.

Centered. Each line of copy is centered on the page. None is aligned vertically on either column edge. Spec marks are the word (**center**) or][.

Centered copy allows for even spacing between letters
and words, as there are no restrictions except the maximum
line length. One shortcoming, however, is that the unde-
fined edges make reading more difficult, which is why
centered copy is generally used only for short copy such
as headlines, advertisements, or invitations. The lines of
this paragraph are centered.

It is best to center lines optically rather than mechanically. Optical centering on lines of type that have quotation marks at the beginning and at the end is especially recommended.

Asymmetrical. When there is no predictable pattern for line endings, the copy is either typed on a page exactly as it should appear typeset line for line, or is typed in a regular manner but interrupted by a hand-drawn Z at the exact place where each typeset line should break. The formula instruction is LL (meaning set line for line).

EXAMPLE: This line Z is marked for Z asymmetrical breaking.

This line

is marked for

asymmetrical breaking.

Wraparound. What an inexperienced proofreader might initially judge as a bad rag or "hole" could simply be a wraparound margin. Pay close attention to copy specs and to the artist's layout. A wraparound is used to follow the outline of a photograph or illustration. Spec mark is the word (wraparound) or (wrap) or (runaround) , usually accompanied by specific dimensions and a precise spacing layout.

> The proofreader should pay close attention to the rag created by the wraparound, as an unattractive marginal rag, space gaps, and too many hyphenated words can result if the artist did not copyfit before the type was set. Most artists will at least furnish the typesetter (and the proofreader) dimensions in picas of the space where type is not to be set. An alternative to precise pica measurement of each line in the wraparound is an outline or drawing of the copy block, including the pattern and dimensions of the wraparound area. If the wraparound does not fit as smoothly as the artist wants, often the writer will change a word here and there for a nicer fit.

Margin Rag. The rag is the pattern created by the line endings on all unjustified margins. While there is no consensus on what a good rag should look like, there are some generally accepted guidelines that the proofreader should follow, unless instructed otherwise.

The main function of type is to be read. A good, marginal rag in the body copy contributes to a smoother read. And although headlines and subheadlines usually break after a thought or for sense, visual appeal of the rag is also a consideration.

A good rag evokes rhythm. It does not call attention to itself. It weaves in and out, its lines alternately short and long, but not varying in length more than 2 ems. A good rag avoids a sharply defined pattern or consecutive lines that are the same length and give the impression of justified copy. A good rag also avoids word breaks on consecutive lines, when possible.

(Bad rag)
It is the rare body of typeset copy that has an
ideal rag throughout, and rarely on the first typesetting
attempt. The rag depends upon the combined efforts
of the artist, an experienced typesetter, and a knowledgeable
proofreader, plus a whole array of other
factors (the typeface, line length, the amount of
space allocated for the copy). A good
typesetter can often adjust bad margin rags, but conscientious
artists do not leave it all to chance. For unless each character
has been counted (by copyfitting) so that the words
will fall exactly where the artist envisions, there could be
some disappointments. Even after careful planning,
it may be necessary to move copy or adjust spacing to achieve
the best results. Good rags take planning and time.

(Better rag)
It is the rare body of typeset copy that has an ideal rag
throughout, and rarely on the first typesetting attempt. The
rag depends upon the combined efforts of the artist, an
experienced typesetter, and a knowledgeable proofreader, plus
a whole array of other factors (the typeface, line length, the
amount of space allocated for the copy). A good typesetter
can often adjust bad margin rags, but conscientious artists do
not leave it all to chance. For unless each character has been
counted (by copyfitting) so that the words will fall exactly
where the artist envisions, there could be some disappointments. Even after careful planning, it may be necessary to
move copy or adjust spacing to achieve the best results. Good
rags take planning and time.

Whatever the proofreader's preference in rag pattern, you will be guided by the artist's instructions. Some may specify a rag with no word breaks, which guarantees an irregular rag.

There will be wide gaps of white space on the ragged margin edge.

Others may specify a rag that looks almost justified. And, as it does in justified copy, this will create irregular letter and word spacing and increase the chances of abrupt line endings. Word breaks at line endings also will occur more often. Sometimes spacing and word breaks can be adjusted by the typesetter with the aid of proofreader instructions. But spacing and word-break problems may often be unavoidable unless the actual copy is changed line by line.

Rags that create fewer spacing problems and word breaks are centered copy rags or rags in copy set flush left, rag right. The hardest rags to correct are in copy that resemble justified and copy set flush right, rag left.

Word Breaks are another marginal consideration. There is some basic agreement on the subject among those who work with type:

▶ Avoid incorrect word divisions.

▶ Avoid word breaks on two or more consecutive lines of type.

▶ Avoid breaks at the beginning of a page or column.

▶ Avoid breaks at the bottom of a page or column.

▶ Avoid two-letter breaks or short word breaks.

▶ Avoid breaks on a hyphenated word or before a dash.

▶ Avoid proper noun breaks.

The rule that is always observed (except in newspaper copy) is the first one. Incorrect word breaks must never be allowed. And many other breaks can be avoided, such as two-letter breaks at the end of a line that could be broken at the next syllable. This often solves a bad margin rag, as well. While there are some basic guides to word division, remember that there are exceptions to almost every rule. Even dictionaries can disagree on syllables. Before marking your correction, consult a dictionary, maybe even two.

The other rules should be followed when possible. The proofreader should question all undesirable breaks, even if you see no solution. The writer or artist may want to avoid the bad break as much as you do and may rewrite or reposition that part of the copy. On the other hand, necessity may sometimes dictate a deviation from the rules (except incorrect word divisions) if the copy cannot be changed to avoid a bad break or if the break makes a better marginal rag.

The in-text mark for a bad word break is to circle the word, then write out the entire word, in syllables, in the margin. Or, separate the word at the correct break with a $\rule{1em}{0pt}$ ⌐ $\rule{1em}{0pt}$ mark inside the copy.

THE MECHANICAL

After the copy is typeset, it is usually returned to the artist (and proofreader) in "chunks," not in the order in which it will appear in print. Copy of the same size or the same typeface is chunked on one galley proof. Headline copy that is typeset on a Typositor is chunked on another galley proof.

Following the checklist for typeset copy (see Appendix B), the proofreader will first read the typeset (live) copy—reader's proof—against the typed (dead) copy, then re-read the live copy until all errors have been found and corrected. When corrections have been made by the typesetter and approved by the proofreader and artist, a glossy, camera-ready print of the corrected type will be made by the typesetter and sent to the artist. The print is commonly called a Velox®[6], Photostat®[7], or "stat." In the artist's studio, the stat will be cut apart and re-assembled, using the artist's layout (comp) as the guide, then attached with rubber cement, wax, or spray adhesive on a mechanical board.

If halftone photos are to be part of the layout, a space (window) is left for each of them on the mechanical. There are several ways to mark halftone art on the mechanical. A black holding line or red acetate inside the window will outline the exact size and position of the halftone. Or a stat with a matte finish, a photograph, or a simple line drawing can be used to indicate the size, cropping, and position of the artwork. None of these can be photographed by the printer's camera. They will be glued, in position, on the mechanical. Written over them will be instructions to the printer: "For Position Only (FPO). Strip In Halftone." Halftone art will be photographed separately by the printer.

---

[6] Velox is a registered trademark of Eastman Kodak Corporation.

[7] Photostat is a registered trademark of Itek Graphic Products.

An overlay, usually a sheet of tracing paper or vellum, will be placed over the mechanical after paste-up. This protects the type and provides a writing area if corrections or additional instructions to the studio are necessary.

The proofreader should inspect the mechanical carefully, reading it again against the dead copy, then comparing it against the layout to make sure all the elements are included and are in place. Follow the proofreading checklist for mechanicals (see Appendix B). Inspect each element for broken type or smudges and dust picked up by careless gluing. Any imperfections on the mechanical will be photographed. They will appear on the negative and become a permanent part of the printing plate. Check the windows on the mechanical, making sure they are the right size and are positioned and placed correctly. When there are names of people listed in the captions under the photos, they should be properly identified and in the same sequence as in the photograph.

All proofreader corrections or notes concerning the mechanical should be written lightly with a nonreproducing pen or a lead pencil on the tissue. Even a pencil impression on the tissue can leave a crease on the typeset copy underneath, if you are not careful. Don't mark on the Velox or Photostat, even with a nonreproducing pen.

After the mechanical has been corrected and returned to you for final inspection, make sure the tissue with your corrections is returned to you, as well. Otherwise you may not remember what you marked on the mechanical, and you will have to read the entire copy again.

A stamp, as in Table 8-1, should be imprinted on the back of the mechanical once it is complete. The back of the mechanical should be signed and dated by each of those responsible for the project.

If there are any subsequent changes after you have approved a mechanical, you should inspect the changes and initial the back of the mechanical before it goes to the printer.

When all the corrections have been made and approved, the old tissue will be replaced with a clean one, ready for instructions to the printer.

TABLE 8-1. MECHANICAL STAMP
Job #_____ Date_____
Studio_____
Proofreader_____
Art_____
Copy_____
Creative Dir._____
Acct. Exec._____
Client_____

PRINTER'S PROOF

The printer receives the mechanical with either separate instructions or instructions written on the tissue. A halftone negative of the mechanical is made. The artwork will undergo a separate process at the printer's before it appears together with the typeset copy. The printer will then place the negatives of the artwork into position on the negative of the mechanical. This is called "stripping in." A printing plate is made, and the actual printing process is ready to begin. At first, only a few copies are made. These printer's proofs, also called press proofs, bluelines, or brownlines, are sent to the customer for inspection. Although not of the same quality as final print will be, the proof is an accepted interpretation of how the finished product will appear.

Usually one who is an expert in print production will read the proof for density, color, imperfections in the printing plate, among many other things. The proofreader may be asked to read it to make sure all the elements are in place and that there are no errors that were overlooked at the mechanical art stage (see the checklist for printer's proof in Appendix B). As this proof is only a sample copy made from the negative plate, no extraordinary measures should be taken to protect it. Use an indelible-ink pen to mark errors or blemishes in the copy.

APPENDIX A
THE PROOFREADER'S TOOLS

▶ two 6-inch nontransparent rulers

▶ magnifying glass

▶ fine-line, indelible-ink red pen

▶ nonreproducing pen

▶ lead pencil

▶ pica and point gauge

▶ dictionaries

▶ grammar/punctuation books

▶ word usage references

▶ stylebook or style sheet

▶ proofreader's marks

▶ world atlas

▶ foreign language dictionary

▶ trade names reference

▶ thesaurus or synonym finder

▶ typeface guides

▶ graphic arts books

APPENDIX B
PROOFREADING CHECKLISTS

TYPED COPY

First Reading

Read the instructions.

Compare with original text—deviations from text, doubly typed words, typographical errors, and incorrect word breaks.

Second Reading

Begin compiling your style sheet.

Read for content—fact or format inconsistency, word usage, sentence structure, subject and verb agreement, repetition of thought or phrases, and incorrect math.

Check the language mechanics—capitalization, punctuation, spelling, grammar, hyphenations and word breaks; legal mandates, footnotes, bibliographies, table of contents, index, tables, and charts.

Third Reading

Check the overall format—type size, margins, alignment, spacing, positioning (headlines, subheads, copy, footnotes, indentations), pagination, clean typing, and general appearance.

Fourth Reading

Read for completeness and perfect copy.

Compare with your style sheet notes.

If the copy is retyped, it should be read again by the proofreader.

TYPESET COPY

First Reading

Compare with dead copy (never from the artist's layout)—deviations from text, doubly typeset words, typographical errors, incorrect word breaks, pairs of quote marks and parenthesis marks.

Second Reading

Follow the type specifications—check typeface and font (weight, width, posture, and size), leading, copy depth, line length, paragraph indentations, column margins (rags), alignment (vertical and horizontal), and centering.

Third Reading

Look at size and placement of rules, dashes, hyphens, and bullets; widows and orphans; page sequence; page and line breaks; letter and word spacing; consecutive word breaks; dirty copy or broken letters; and type density.

Fourth Reading

A final read for completeness of copy, including headlines, subheads, captions, legal information, and footnotes.

When marking typeset copy, remember to mark (PE) (printer's error) or (AA) (author's alteration) beside each correction or change. Printer's errors will be corrected without any charge, but author's alterations will be charged to your company.

After corrections have been made by the typesetter, read the entire copy again, if you can. Words or entire lines can be dropped from the bottom of a page, margins can become misaligned—many things can happen. If there is no time to read it all, at least re-read a line or two above and below the line where the correction was made (as well as the corrected line, of course). Watch for new word breaks, line breaks, and page breaks. Double-check the table of contents to make sure it is consistent with the newly corrected copy. Indexing should also be checked again by the editor or proofreader.

If the copy is re-typeset, it should be read again by the proofreader.

THE MECHANICAL

First Reading

Compare with dead copy—final check for typos and deviations from original text; inclusion of all copy elements including headlines, subheads, captions, footnotes, tables, lists, legends, logos, photos, legal information, trademarks, and copyright line.

Second Reading

Review type specifications and artist's instructions to studio; check for uniform positioning and alignment of all elements (numbers, headlines, subheads, and captions); watch for uneven, crowded, or loose spacing; check for broken rules or type, dirty copy, and correct pagination; compare copy against table of contents; and make sure glued elements are securely on board.

Third Reading

Look for overall completeness.

If the copy is repositioned on the mechanical, it should be read again by the proofreader.

PRINTER'S PROOF

It is always a safeguard to read the printer's proof against the original text, even if the mechanical was carefully inspected. The proofreader should review the proof, comparing it against the artist's layout to make sure none of the elements dropped off the mechanical before the plate was made. Watch for the following: inconsistent leading and alignment, positioning of the elements, missing elements, spacing, type density, dirty places on the proof, and broken copy. If changes are made, they should be marked (PE) or (AA) .

PUBLISHED WORKS

It is the masochistic proofreader who reads again at this stage. Finding an error too late only adds to the anxiety of an already nerve-wracking occupation. When the proofreader sees the article or advertisement in final print, the page should be quickly turned. If there is an error, it will undoubtedly be caught and reported to you by someone whose own errors you correct daily. Don't go looking for trouble.

APPENDIX C
WORDS AND PHRASES
COMMONLY CONFUSED
OR MISUSED

a, an
abrogate, abdicate
accept, except
ad, add
adapt, adopt
admission, admittance
adverse, averse
advert, avert
advice, advise
affect, effect
aid, aide
all ready, already
all together, altogether
alley, ally

allude, elude
alter, altar
ambiguous, ambivalent
amend, emend
amoral, immoral
amuse, bemuse
anecdote, antidote
ante-, anti-
appraise, apprise
assassin, murderer
assay, essay
audience, spectators,
   congregation
avoid, evade

baited, bated
bare, bear
bazaar, bizarre
beside, besides
better than, more than
between, among
blatant, flagrant
bloc, block
boat, ship
born, borne
bough, bow
brake, break
breach, breech
breadth, breath, breathe
bring, take
burglary, robbery
calendar, calender
cannon, canon
canvas, canvass
capacity, capability
capital, capitol
censer, censor
ceremonial, ceremonious
cession, session
chafe, chaff
childish, childlike
chord, cord
cite, sight, site
classic, classical
climactic, climatic
clinch, clench
compare to, compare with
complimentary,
   complementary

comprehensible,
   comprehensive
comprise, compose
confute, refute
connote, denote
consul, council, counsel
contemptible, contemptuous
continual, continuous
convince, persuade
corps, corpse
could care less, couldn't care
   less
credible, creditable,
   credulous
criteria, criterion
dairy, diary
delusion, illusion
deprecate, depreciate
desert, dessert
diagnosis, prognosis
different from, different
   than
discomfit, discomfort
discreet, discrete
disinterested, uninterested
dispute, refute
distinct, distinctive
dual, duel
effective, effectual
egoism, egotism
elegy, eulogy
elicit, illicit
emigrate, immigrate
energize, enervate

ensure, insure, assure

enthused, enthusiastic

equable, equitable

ever so often, every so often

farther, further

faze, phase

fewer, less

flagrant, blatant

flail, flay

flair, flare

flaunt, flout

flounder, founder

forceful, forcible

foreword, forward

fortuitous, fortunate

gamble, gambol

got, gotten

grisly, grizzly

hangar, hanger

hanged, hung

hardly, scarcely

hardy, hearty

he/she/I, him/her/me

historic, historical

hyper-, hypo-

i.e., e.g.

I/you, myself/yourself

idle, idol

if I were, if I was

illusion, allusion, delusion

imminent, eminent,
  immanent

implicit, explicit

impracticable, impractical

imply, infer

in behalf of, on behalf of

in, into

incident, incidence

incite, insight

incredible, incredulous

indict, indite

ingenious, ingenuous

intense, intensive

inter-, intra-

its, it's

judicial, judicious

lagoon, cove

lay, lie

lead, led

leave, let

lesser, lessor

lighted, lit

lightening, lightning

like, such as

loan, lend

loath, loathe

loose, lose

luxuriant, luxurious

masterful, masterly

material, materiel

mean, median

metal, medal, meddle

militate, mitigate

miner, minor

moral, morale

mutual, common

nauseous, nauseated

navel, naval

noisome, noisy
official, officious
or, nor, neither
oral, verbal
ordinance, ordnance
orient, orientate
palate, palette, pallet
passed, past
peace, piece
peaceful, peaceable
pedal, peddle, petal
periodic, periodical
perquisite, prerequisite
persecute, prosecute
perspective, prospective
pertinent, pertaining
plain, plane
practical, practicable
practically, virtually
prescribe, proscribe
presume, assume
pretext, pretense
principal, principle
pro-, pre-
proceed, precede
prophecy, prophesy
prostate, prostrate
proven, proved
quite, quiet
regardless, irregardless
respectively, respectfully
revenge, avenge
rise, raise

role, roll
sanitarium, sanitorium
scraggly, scraggy, spindly
seasonable, seasonal
sensual, sensuous
shear, sheer
sit, set
stationary, stationery
than, then
their, there, they're
this kind, these kinds
titled, entitled
to, too, two
tortuous, torturous
trail, trial
transient, transitory
trooper, trouper
try to, try and
turbid, turgid
unexceptionable,
   unexceptional
usage, use
use to, used to
valued, valuable
vein, vane
venal, venial
weather, whether
when, where
which, that
who's, whose
who, whom
your, you're

APPENDIX D
GENERAL OFFICE STYLE
SHEET

(This is for a fictitious consulting firm, the clients being city and county governments.)

FORMAT

▶ Unless otherwise noted, format assumes vertical spacing of six lines per inch.

▶ Examples of the following are attached to the style sheet.

Letters—Elements and Spacing between Elements

Heading or letterhead   Date
   (3 blank lines)   (3 blank lines)

Address   Complimentary close
   (2 blank lines)   (4 blank lines)

Reference lines   Signature
   (2 blank lines)   (2 blank lines)

Salutation   Stenographic reference
   (1 blank line)   (1 blank line)

Body   Enclosures
   (1 blank line)

Notes:

▶ All lines are set flush with the left margin.

▶ Paragraphs are not indented.

▶ There is one blank line between paragraphs.

Long Letters

      Left/right margins: $1''/1''$
                 Tabs: $0.5''$
         Top margins: 1st page, $1.5''$; 2nd page, $1''$
    Bottom margin: $1''$
              Paper: Standard engraved letterhead

Note:

▶ On letters longer than one page, type "Page _____ of _____" one-half inch (three lines) from the bottom of the page.

Short Letters

      Left/right margins: $1''/1''$
                 Tabs: $0.5''$
  Top/bottom margins: Centered vertically on page
              Paper: Standard engraved letterhead

Envelopes (Standard Engraved #10)

        Left margin: $3.5''$
         Top margin: $2''$

Notes:

▶ When an address line must be continued on a second line, indent the second line two spaces.

▶ Suite, room, or apartment numbers follow the street address on the same line.

Reports to Clients—Elements and Style

Left/right margins:	1.5″ on edge to be bound; 1″ on other edge
Title page:	Position to match cutout in report cover.
Table of contents:	Top/bottom margins—1st page, 1.5″; subsequent pages, 1″
List of figures:	Top/bottom margins—1st page, 1.5″; subsequent pages, 1″
Chapter title page:	Top/bottom margins—1.5″/1″
All other pages:	Top/bottom margins—1″/1″
Paragraphs:	Indent 0.5″, no space between paragraphs
Page numbering:	Style—table of contents through list of figures, lowercase Roman numerals; body of report, continuous Arabic numerals
	Location—center of page, 1/2″ from bottom
	If printing both sides of page, insert blank pages if necessary to start each chapter on an odd page number.
Endnotes:	Superscripted Arabic numerals
Paper:	20# "client" bond

Memos

Left/right margins:	1″/1″
Tabs:	0.5″
Top margins:	1st page, 1.5″; 2nd page, 1″
Bottom margin:	1″
Paper:	1st page—preprinted memo form; 2nd page—standard bond

TYPE STYLE
Epson LQ Series Printers

Reports to clients:	Roman 12 pt. (PS)
Memos:	Roman (12 CPI)
Long letters:	Roman 12 pt. (PS)
Short letters:	Roman 12 pt. (PS)
Envelopes:	Roman 12 pt. (PS)

GENERAL STYLE ELEMENTS

Dates

▶ June 1, 1991

▶ June 1991

▶ Summer 1989

Numerals

▶ Spell one through nine; numerals from 10 on.

▶ 3%, not three % or three percent.

▶ 99%, not ninety-nine % or ninety-nine percent.

Punctuation

▶ Put titles of speeches in quotes.

▶ Underline names of books and newspapers.

CAPITALIZATION/HYPHENATION/ITALICS/ POSSESSIVES/PUNCTUATION/SPELLING

(adj) adjective

(cn) collective noun

(dict) dictionary

(n) noun

(pa) predicate adj.

(pl) plural

(poss) possessive

(sing) singular

(v) verb

A

B

▶ Brzezinski, Wertmüller, and Velázquez, Engineers

C

▶ the city (other than client city)

▶ the City (client city)

▶ City of Chicago

▶ the county (other than client county)

▶ the County (client county)

▶ cul-de-sacs (pl)

D

▶ Department of Community Affairs (DCA)

▶ Department of Natural Resources (DNA)

▶ data base (n)

▶ database (adj.)

▶ DeKalb County

▶ Department of Housing and Urban Development (HUD)

▶ drafting film (do not use trade name)

E

F

▶ Federal government

▶ fee-simple (adj.)

G

H

▶ House Bill 215

I

▶ IL (Illinois, in addresses)

▶ Ill. 34 (Illinois State Highway 34)

J

K

L

▶ the Legislature (client's state)

M

▶ the Midwest

▶ multi-family (adj.)

N

O

P

▶ Ph.D.'s (pl)

Q

R

▶ Robinson and Associates

S

▶ Senate Bill 14

▶ the Soil Erosion Control Act

T

▶ tax-exempt (adj.)

▶ townhouse (n)(adj.)

UV

WXYZ

▶ the Zoning Ordinance (client's ordinance)

MISCELLANEOUS

APPENDIX E
MANUSCRIPT STYLE SHEET

(Manuscript)

America Discovers Its Wilderness

Until the early 20th century, wilderness survived only as a byproduct of the movement to reserve public lands for other purposes. Then the Forest Service began experimenting in the early 1920's.

Arthur Carhart, the agency's first landscape architect, helped preserve the Trappers' Lake Region in Colorado from development, and Aldo Leopold, in 1924, created the Gila Wilderness in New Mexico, the first official wilderness area in the United States.

Wilderness Inventory

Chief Forester William Greeley ordered inventories of all undeveloped National Forest lands larger than 230,400 acres

in 1926. Soon after, rules were established for managing
"primitive areas." By the mid-1930's the agency had
designated nearly 14 million acres of primitive land.

The leading advocate of wilderness preservation in the
1930's was Bob Marshall, who in 1937 became head of
Recreation and Lands for the Forest Service. In 1939 Chief
Forester Ferdinand Silcox approved Marshall's plan to
inventory, study, and reclassify primitive lands as wilderness
areas to provide them greater protection. . . .

Wild and Scenic Rivers Act

Congress passed the Wild and Scenic Rivers Act in 1968 to
preserve portions of 50 rivers on Federal land in their
free-flowing state. Many additions to this system followed.

The Wilderness Act transferred 9 million acres of
National Forest wilderness land into the wilderness system
and required review of the 5 million acres of remaining
primitive land for possible inclusion. Beyond the scope of the
Wilderness Act were millions of acres of undesignated but
undeveloped land in the National Forests that were also
potential wildernesses. . . .

Eastern Wilderness Areas

Almost all the eastern National Forests had been created
from cut-over and partially roaded land and, although many
of the forests had grown back, none of them were as pristine
as the forests of the West. The Forest Service wanted to create
a separate "Wild Areas" System in the 1970's for eastern
areas, arguing that the Wilderness Act did not allow inclusion
of cut-over areas. . . . [8]

---

[8] Dennis Roth. "America Discovers Its Wilderness," *Our American Land*. U.S. Government
Printing Office: 1987. Pp. 77–79.

STYLE SHEET: AMERICA DISCOVERS ITS WILDERNESS		
CAPITALIZATION **HYPHENATION** **ITALICS** **POSSESSIVE** **PUNCTUATION** **SPELLING** (n) noun (v) verb (adj) adjective (pa) predicate adj (cn) collective noun (pl) plural (poss) possessive (sing) singular (dict) dictionary	**A** agency	**B** byproduct

C
Arthur Carhart
Chief Forester
Congress
cut-over (adj)
	D
	Dates
	20th century
	mid-1930's
		E
		eastern
		East
		Eastern
		   Wilderness Act
		   (so-called)

F Forest Service Federal	**G** Gila Wilderness William Greeley	**H**

I	J	K

L	M	N

Aldo Leopold	Bob Marshall
	
	Multiple Use-
	  Sustained
	  Yield Act of
	  1960
	
	Midwest
		Numbers
		
		all-numerical
		  style
		
		14 million
		
		National
		  Forest(s)
		
		Northeast

O	P	Q

R	S	T
Recreation and Lands roaded (adj.) reclassify/ reclassification	South Ferdinand Silcox	Trapper's Lake Region

U-V	W	X-Y-Z
	Wild and Scenic Rivers Act (1968) Wilderness Act West the Wilderness Society (the Society) "Wild Areas" System	

MISCELLANEOUS FACTS/NOTES

STYLE
initial-cap head, bold face, centered
initial-cap subhead (lowercase articles, prepositions, conjunctions), book weight, flush left
flush left first paragraph under subhead, indent following paragraphs 3 ems
comma before <u>and</u> in series
line endings—no word breaks
Triumvirate typeface, 11/16 × 24. + 5 before subs

APPENDIX F
CLIENT STYLE SHEET

THE CITIZENS AND SOUTHERN CORPORATION
The "Corporation"
Subsidiaries of the Corporation
(Note: Indentation indicates subsidiary status.)

CITIZENS AND SOUTHERN GEORGIA CORPORATION
The Citizens and Southern National Bank
Citizens and Southern Capital Corporation
Citizens and Southern Securities Corporation
Citizens and Southern Commercial Corporation
The Ocmulgee Corporation
C&S Real Estate Services, Inc.

Citizens and Southern International Bank
Citizens and Southern International Bank of
New Orleans
Citizens and Southern Mortgage Corporation
CSGA Funding Corporation
C&S Business Credit, Inc.
C&S Capital Corporation
C&S Restaurant Holding Corporation

CITIZENS AND SOUTHERN TRUST COMPANY, INC.

Citizens and Southern Trust Company (Georgia), N.A.
Citizens and Southern Trust Company (South Carolina),
N.A.
Citizens and Southern Trust Company (Florida), N.A.

CITIZENS AND SOUTHERN INSURANCE SERVICES, INC.

THE CITIZENS AND SOUTHERN LIFE INSURANCE COMPANY

CITIZENS AND SOUTHERN INVESTMENT ADVISORS, INC.

C&S FAMILY CREDIT, INC.

C&S Family Credit of Alabama, Inc.
C&S Family Credit of Florida, Inc.
C&S Family Credit of North Carolina, Inc.
C&S Family Credit of Tennessee, Inc.

CITIZENS AND SOUTHERN FLORIDA CORPORATION

The Citizens and Southern National Bank of Florida
First Land Sales, Inc.
Second Land Sales, Inc.

CITIZENS AND SOUTHERN SOUTH CAROLINA CORPORATION

The Citizens and Southern National Bank of
  South Carolina
  Carolina Pacific, Inc.
C&S Financial Services, Inc.
Citizens and Southern Systems, Inc.
Citizens and Southern Realty Corporation
Citizens and Southern Housing Corporation
Carolina Credit Life Insurance Company

USAGE/PLACEMENT

- Registration mark on a C&S service (such as MasterCard®)—once per page.
- C&S logo in box must have registration mark.
- Member(s) FDIC—must be used in ads that mention deposit services; must be used on all TV ads; Seniors Club; do not use on Trust ads.
- Equal Housing Lender logo—use on any ad that mentions real estate or mortgage loans.
- Plural for acronyms is with apostrophe (IRA's, ATM's).

TYPEFACE

- Caledonia—Copy
- Caslon 540—Headline

LEGAL FOR ALL PRINT

- ©1989 The Citizens and Southern Corporation (except Citizens and Southern Insurance Services, Inc.)
- C&S® logo (all print)

TRADEMARK RULES

- Always use as an adjective, modifying a generic or common name for the services. (Money Saver® banking services)
- Do not use as a general descriptive adjective.
- Never use as a verb.

---

[9] The C&S style sheet and materials contained therein are the sole property of The Citizens and Southern Corporation and may not be used without its express permission.

- Never use as a noun. Never: Open a Money Saver® today.
  Use: Open a Money Saver® account today.
- Do not use in possessive form, such as C&S's.
- Do not pluralize a service mark.
- Do not couple service marks.
- In textual material, provide service marks with distinctive appearance by using all capital letters, italics, quotation marks, or different color or size lettering.
- Use proper notice for registered marks by placing a (®) next to the mark.

CAPITALIZATION/HYPHENATION/ITALICS/ POSSESSIVE/PUNCTUATION/SPELLING

(adj) adjective
(cn) collective noun
(dict) dictionary
(n) noun
(pa) predicate adj.

(pl) plural
(poss) possessive
(sing) singular
(v) verb

A

- account officer
- Automatic Teller Card
- American Express® Travelers Cheques
- annuity
- Annuity Hotline
- Answer Center
- asset-based

- Assured Balance Line
- Atlantic Southeast Airlines
- Automated Cash Management
- Automated Teller Machines
- automated teller network
- AVAIL®

B

- Bank-by-Mail
- Bank-by-Phone
- BankCard Center
- Bank 'N Shop Centers
- BANKWINDOW®
- benefits package
- benefits plan

- Better Business Banking services
- Big Saver Account
- Bonus Checking account
- Branch Manager
- buy outs

C

- cardholder
- cashier's checks
- Cash Management Consulting Group
- Cash Management Officer
- Cash Management Services
- Certificates of Deposit (CD)
- Certified Employee Benefit Specialists
- Check Safekeeping
- CIRRUS®
- closely held (adj)
- Commercial Premium Investment Account
- Commercial Telephone Banking

- Common Stock Fund
- Corporate Cash Management
- The C&S Answer Center
- C&S Bank's (poss) (but not C&S's)
- The C&S Business Telephone Banking System
- C&S Consulting Group
- C&S Discount Brokerage
- C&S Executor/Personal Representative
- C&S Family Credit Revolving Account™ (one line)
- C&S Floridian Club
- C&S Market Reviews

- C&S Trust and Financial Officer
- CUSTOM(k)

- Customer Service Representative
- Custom wallet checks

D
- data bases
- disability insurance

E
- the Emerald Account
- energy-efficient (adj)
- energy-saving (adj)

F
- Factor's Chain International (FCI)
- Family Credit Services
- fax
- Federal Depositors Insurance Corporation (FDIC)
- Federal Income Tax Form
- financial specialist
- Financial Wizard℠ machines

- fixed rate
- Fixed Term (IRA)
- Flat Fee Checking
- Florida Instant Banker
- the Floridian Club or Floridian Club or the C&S Floridian Club
- full-cost
- full-service (adj)
- 401(k)

G

- Georgia Newcomer Hotline 1-800-555-7291
- Gold Coast (Florida)
- Gold Reserve
- Government Banking Division
- Government Banking Services
- Green Pages directory

H

- HONOR^{SM}

I

- Income Fund
- Individual Market Investment Account
- Instant Banker (n)
- Instant Banker(s)** (see Misc. Facts)
- Instant Banker Machine
- Instant Banker transaction
- Instant Banking Card
- Do not use Instant Banking as a noun
- InstantCheck Debit Card
- Instant Checking
- Instant Money Loan
- Insurance Services
- INSURED MUNICIPALS INCOME TRUST™
- interest bearing (adj)
- interest checking account
- Investment Advisors
- IRA (see Misc. Facts)

J

K

- KEOGH's (pl)

L

- Loan Pack
- lock box

M

- MasterCard®
- MasterCard® II
- MasterCard® gold card
- MasterCard II® InstantCheck Card (see InstantCheck Debit Card)
- MasterTeller®
- Market Investment (IRA)
- Market Investment Account
- Market Investment Account Instant Check (not Accounts)
- Market Line account
- Market Reviews
- Master Trust
- Master Trust Department
- Master Trustee
- Master Trust services
- MIA/IRA
- Minimum Balance Checking
- MoneyLine®***
- MoneyLine® Reserve
- money market (adj) (noun)***
- Money Saver® account***
- Money Saver® Checking***
- mutual funds

N

- Newcomer Guide
- Newcomer Hotline 1-800-555-7291
- Newcomer Kit
- Newcomer Services
- no-obligation (adj)
- NOW Checking (no ®)

O

- C&S Operations Group

P
- The Peoples Bank of Carrollton
- Personal Access Number
- Personal Banker
- Personal Trust Officer
- policyholders
- Portfolio Evaluation Services
- Preferred MasterCard®
- Premium Investment Account
- Public Finance Division

Q

R
- Ready Equity Account (home equity loan)
- Ready Equity Center
- Ready Reserve
- Regular Business Checking
- regular checking
- C&S Relationship Manager
- resell
- R-values (n)
- Revolving Account™ (see C)

S
- safe deposit boxes**** (see Misc. Facts)
- SCOREBOARD℠
- self-directed (adj)
- Self-Directed (IRA)
- seniors account
- Seniors Club (no apos. in SC, GA, or FL)
- setup
- SIPC
- Sixty Plus Checking
- South Carolina Financial Wizard Machines
- Southeast, South
- Special Situation Funds

T

- TARTAN Plus™ (see Misc. Facts)
- Tax Anticipation Notes (TAN's)
- tax-deferred (adj)
- Tax-Deferred Annuities
- tax-exempt (adj)
- Tax-Exempt Lease
- Telephone Banking System or Telephone Banking
- tellerphone
- telex
- term insurance
- Think of your future with C&S® (copy)
- THINK OF YOUR FUTURE WITH C&S® (logo)
- Time Deposit Account(s)
- Touch-tone® (see Misc. Facts)
- Travel Checking account
- traveler's cheques or traveler's checks
- Travel Dollars
- travel-size bank
- "Trust-Foresters"
- trust officer (or C&S Trust Officer)
- Trust Specialist
- T-shirt (n)
- TUCS® (see Misc. Facts)

U

- universal life
- Unit Investment Trusts
- U.S. Treasury bill rate

V

- Variable Rate (IRA)
- VISA®
- VISA® gold card®
- VISA® Instant Check card
- VISA® Premier

W

- WIZARD℠ banking machine or Financial Wizard℠
- WIZARD℠ Reserve

X

Y

- Your money's worth®

Z

MISCELLANEOUS FACTS/NOTES

- 200 branches all over GA; more than 185 Automated Teller Machines
- 150 branches throughout FL
- 477 branches throughout Southeast (477 employing over 13,687 people)
- 100 years of service (1889-1989)
- TUCS is a registered trademark of Trust Universe Comparison Service.
- Touch-tone is a registered trademark of American Telephone & Telegraph Co.
- The C&S Answer Center—1-800-555-5940 (555-8311 in Columbia)
- 688-RATE
- Seniors Club (55 and older)

- TARTAN Plus is a registered trademark of Recognition Equipment, Inc.
- *IRA—Fixed rate only. Substantial penalties may apply to early withdrawals from time deposits and IRA's.
- **Instant Banker—AVAIL®/CIRRUS® charges apply to use on non-C&S automated teller machines, however.
- ***MoneyLine, money market, Money Saver—Under license of agreements, these marks may not be used outside of designated Southeastern states.
- ****Safe deposit boxes—where available

C&S SECURITIES LOCATIONS

Atlanta

1. Suite 1800
   33 North Avenue, N.E.
   Atlanta, Georgia 30308
   Local: (404) 897-3200
   Nationwide Toll Free: 1-800-241-0446

2. 1 Perimeter Center East, N.E.
   Atlanta, Georgia 30346
   Local: (404) 396-3189
   Nationwide Toll Free: 1-800-438-2434

Augusta

3. C&S National Bank Building
   709 Broad Street
   Augusta, Georgia 30902
   Local: (404) 828-8400
   Georgia Toll Free: 1-800-242-9240
   Southeast Toll Free: 1-800-445-8396

Knoxville

4. Suite 601

First Tennessee Building

530 South Gay Street

Knoxville, Tennessee 37902

Local: (615) 546-4002 Knoxville

(615) 983-2215 Maryville

(615) 483-5185 Oak Ridge

Tennessee Toll Free: 1-800-327-7283

Tampa

5. Westshore Center

Suite 150

1715 North Westshore Boulevard

Tampa, Florida 33607

Local: (813) 879-1911

Florida Toll Free: 1-800-282-5610

Nationwide Toll Free: 1-800-237-4504

Ft. Myers

6. Suite 301

2400 First Street

Ft. Myers, Florida 33901

(located in First National Bank of Ft. Myers)

Local: (813) 335-1333

Florida Toll Free: 1-800-282-5464

Ft. Lauderdale

7. One Financial Plaza

7th Floor

Ft. Lauderdale, Florida 33394

Local: (305) 765-2777

Florida Toll Free: 1-800-433-0002

Florida Corporate

The Citizens and Southern National Bank of Florida
Westshore Center
1715 North Westshore Boulevard
Tampa, Florida 33607
1-813-874-4600

GLOSSARY

alignment, horizontal—the positioning of type on a line so that the x-height of each character rests on a common baseline. (Also called base alignment)

alignment, vertical—the positioning of lines of type where the ends of lines meet at the same point. (Flush left, flush right, or justified)

art—all artwork and photographs; also all original copy to be reproduced.

ascender—the part of the lowercase letters that extends above the x-height (b,d,f,h,k,l,t have ascenders).

author's alteration (AA)—author's change or any other alteration of the manuscript that is not a printer's error.

back slant—type that slants backward, opposite of italic.

bad break (BB)—incorrectly hyphenated word at the end of a typed or typeset line; also when a page or column of type ends on a divided word.

bad copy—any copy that is illegible to the typesetter.

baseline—an imaginary line where all letters rest. Descenders will be below the baseline.

bleed—excess area required on engravings to extend the printed image beyond the trimmed edges of a page.

blueline (or brownline)—a preliminary printer's proof for inspection purposes.

body type—text type used for reading, not display.

boldface (bf)—term designating a typeface weight that is black and heavy.

book type—same as body or text type; used for the text or main body of a printed piece.

border—decorative line surrounding a typographic area.

broken rule—a broken line; also called leaders.

broken type—type that has not reproduced distinctly and looks broken in places.

bullet—a dot of any size used to itemize or for ornamental purposes.

cap height—the height of a capital letter from its base to the top of the letter.

caps (or uppercase)—capital letters of the alphabet.

caps and lowercase (or initial caps) (c&lc or u&lc)—the first letter of a word is capitalized, the remaining letters lowercase; or the first letter of every word in a series is capitalized, the remaining letters lowercase.

caps and small caps (c&sc)—two sizes of capital letters on one typeface. The small caps are usually two-thirds the height of capital letters.

caption (or cutline)—explanatory text that accompanies an illustration or photograph.

centered—a line or lines of type set centered on a page or column.

characters per pica (CPP)—the number of average type characters that will fit in one pica space.

chunk—to typeset a word or a portion of copy, but not in the order in which it was written.

column rule—rule used to separate columns of type.

comparison reading—two pieces of copy are compared to make sure they are identical.

comprehensive (or comp or dummy)—a layout (LO) showing the exact position of all elements: headlines, subheads, body copy, photographs, line art, logos. Used as a reference for building a mechanical, the comprehensive may be rough or elaborate.

condensed—a type width specification in which the letters are condensed in width, but not in height.

copy—manuscript before it is printed; also all typewritten material, photos, and illustrations before they are printed.

copyfitting—a mathematical procedure to determine the area required to typeset a given amount of copy in a specified typeface.

copyholder—one who reads the dead copy aloud to the proofreader.

crop marks (or register marks)—crosses or other marks used to position photographs or copy on a board before printing.

cursive—typefaces that resemble handwriting.

cut—to eliminate.

cutline—see *caption*.

dead copy—the original manuscript or a proofread, typed version of the manuscript used to compare against typeset versions.

density—the degree of darkness of type or any other photographic image.

descender—that part of the lowercase letters that extends below the baseline (g,j,p,q,y have descenders).

dirty copy—type that is smudged from handling or spotted with ink or glue.

display type—larger, bolder, or more decorative type than that usually used in body text. Primarily used for headlines.

do not set (DNS)—instruction to the typesetter not to set a word or words included in the copy.

dry reading—see *noncomparison reading.*

dummy—see *comprehensive.*

edit—to check for facts, word usage, spelling, grammar, punctuation, and consistency of style. May be part of the proofreader's duties.

em quad—a square of space of a given type size. Used to measure indentations and dashes.

engraver (or printer)—a broad term for one who prints.

engraving—a broad term for any form of printing.

en quad—the same depth as an em-quad, but one-half the width. Used to measure indentations and dashes.

extended type (or expanded)—opposite of condensed type. Characters are wider than the normal design of the typeface.

face—a full range of type of the same design. Also the surface of a body of type that makes an impression; the impression itself; the size or style of a letter or character in the type.

family—a range of typeface designs that are all variations of one basic style. The usual components of a type family are roman, italic, and bold. These can also vary in width (condensed or extended) and in weight (light to extra bold). Some type families have many versions.

flush left or right—copy that is set to align vertically at the left or the right. When margins are both flush left and flush right, the type is called justified.

flush paragraph—a paragraph with no indentations.

font—a complete set or assortment of characters in one size and one typeface. Usually contains all of the upper- and lowercase letters, as well as punctuation marks, numerals, ligatures, and other characters.

footnote—note appearing at the bottom of a page, referring to information given somewhere on that page.

format—general term for style, size, and overall appearance of a printed piece.

for positioning only (FPO)—term used on a mechanical to indicate where a photograph or drawing will be positioned.

galley proof (or reader's proof)—a rough proof of type, usually not assembled, for inspection purposes to make sure the type is properly set.

gauge—commonly called a line gauge or a pica rule. A metal or plastic ruler calibrated in picas on one edge and inches on the other. Transparent rulers that may also be calibrated in points. Used to measure type.

Gothic—black letter type resembling hand-drawn letters of the early scribes, or sans serif type (in U.S.).

gradation—the range of tones in art, negatives, and reproductions.

greek—disarranged or jumbled type sometimes used in a proposed layout for the purpose of counting characters or to judge type appearance.

gutter—blank space where two pages meet at the binding, or blank space between the columns of type.

hairline—usually refers to a rule (line) measuring 1/4-point wide; also the thin stroke of serif type.

halftone—the printing image formed by dots of varying size when a negative is made through a halftone screen. Any photograph in a magazine, newspaper, or brochure is a halftone.

hanging bullets—an arrangement of type in which all bullets are set flush left (or right) and all lines of copy that follow are indented.

hanging indentation—the first line of copy is set full measure and all the lines that follow are indented.

hanging punctuation—primarily in justified copy when hyphens, periods, or other punctuation marks at the end of the line of type are moved just outside the margin. Used for aesthetic purposes.

headline (or head)—title of an article or advertisement.

head margin—the white space above the first line on a page.

indentation (also indention)—blank spaces at the beginning of a typeset line.

indicia—identifying marks or indications.

initial caps—the first letter of every word is capitalized.

italic—a style of type that slants to the right.

justified type—each line of type is set exactly the same length.

kern—to adjust the space between letters or words, usually meaning to tighten.

kill—to delete unwanted copy.

layout—see *comprehensive.*

lead or leading (or line space)—the amount of space, measured in points, between lines of typeset copy. Lines without leading are referred to as solid type. Also measured space between typeset letters and words.

leaders—rows of dashes (rules) or dots (bullets) used to guide the eye across the page.

lead-in—first few words in a block of copy set in a different, contrasting typeface.

legal lines—mandatory copy such as trademarks, service marks, and copyright notices.

letter spacing—spacing between the individual letters.

ligature (lig)—a character of type, such as fi and fl, combining two or more letters.

lightface (lf)—a lighter version of a standard typeface weight.

line art—headlines, body copy, captions, decorative devices, and drawings that contain only black and white with no gray tones.

line for line (LL or L/L)—instructions to the typesetter to set line lengths exactly as they appear on the manuscript.

line height—the measure of a line of type plus the leading.

line length—maximum line length of the copy, measured in picas.

line space—see *lead.*

link—the stroke connecting the top and bottom of a lowercase *g.*

logotype (or logo)—the name, symbol, or trademark of a company.

loop—the lower portion of the lowercase roman *g.*

lowercase (lc)—refers to letters or words that are not capitalized.

margins—the areas around type and illustrations that are not printed.

markup—to mark type specifications on the original copy.

measure—the length of the line that is to be typeset.

mechanical (or keyline or paste-up)—camera-ready paste-up on a board of all type and design elements in the exact position they are to be printed. The mechanical also contains instructions, either in the margin or on a tissue overlay, for the printer.

minus (or negative) letter spacing or word spacing—reduction of the normal space between letter characters or words.

mutton—expression for em space.

negative—a photographic image on film or glass on which color values are reversed.

noncomparison (or dry) reading—a single piece of copy is proofread and there is no other copy to compare it against.

nonreproducing—usually refers to a special pen or pencil whose impressions are invisible when copy is duplicated or printed.

nut—expression for en space.

offset—the most common method of printing.

orphan—the first line of a paragraph when it appears alone at the bottom of a page; also the last line of a paragraph when it appears at the top of a page.

out, see copy (OSC)—instruction to the typesetter that some of the original copy has not been typeset.

outline—a line on the outside edge of letters on a display typeface.

paste-up—see *mechanical.*

Photostat (or stat)—trade name for a photoprint, commonly placed on mechanicals to indicate size, cropping, and position of artwork. Also see *Velox.*

phototypesetting—projection of type characters onto photosensitive film or paper.

pic—a photograph.

pica—print measurement for length and depth of copy. 6 picas = 1 inch; 12 points = 1 pica.

pica rule (or line gauge)—a tool used for measuring picas.

point—print measurement for type size, paragraph indentations, and dash measurement. 72 points = 1 inch; 12 points = 1 pica.

point gauge—a tool for measuring points.

positive letter spacing or word spacing—an increase in the normal space used between letter characters or words.

posture—the slant of a typeface.

printer—general term referring to anyone working in the printing trade, including typesetters or typographers.

printer's error (PE)—an error made by the typesetter or printer in production.

proof (or printout, hard copy)—a sample sheet of printed material that is checked and corrected against the original manuscript. Also see *reader's proof* and *repro proof.*

proofreader—a person who reads the typed or typeset copy against the original manuscript to make sure it is typographically correct.

proofreader's marks—shorthand symbols used to indicate alterations or corrections in the copy. The symbols are standard throughout the communications and printing industry.

query—a question concerning the copy by the proofreader to the editor, the writer, the typesetter, or the printer.

rag—the side margins of typeset copy.

ragged type—copy with uneven margins left or right.

reader's proof (or reader's)—a sample copy of typeset material for proofreading and on which corrections are made.

repro proof—a fine-quality proof used in reproduction.

roman—type in which the upright strokes are vertical (as distinguished from italic in which the strokes are slanted).

Roman—term often used to describe serif type.

rule—a black line used for a number of typographic effects, including boxes and borders.

run—to print.

runaround—see *wraparound*.

run in—to set type with no paragraph breaks or to insert new copy without making a new paragraph.

running page—a book title or chapter head repeated at the top of every page in a book.

sans serif—typefaces that do not have serifs.

script—type resembling handwriting or writing with a brush.

serif—line projecting from the top or bottom of a main stroke in letters of some typefaces.

service mark—a name, symbol, or other device identifying a service officially registered and legally restricted to the use of the owner.

shoulder—curved stroke of the *h, m,* and *n.*

sic (or *cq* or *ok*)—marginal note to the reader or typesetter that an unusual word, which might ordinarily be queried, is an approved spelling.

size—the measure of a typeface in points.

slick—a high-quality, camera-ready enamel proof.

solid type—lines of type with no leading.

specs—see *type specifications*.

spine—curved stroke of an *S* or *s*.

stat—see *photostat*.

stet—a proofreader's mark that indicates copy marked for correction should stand as it was before the correction was made.

straight copy—type not accompanied by display materials such as photographs or drawings.

stress—the direction or thickening in a curved stroke of a letter.

studio—an artist's workroom, usually where the mechanical is prepared.

stylebook or style sheet—an orderly listing of style points to which the manuscript must conform.

subscript (also inferior)—a small symbol, letter, or number that prints below and to the side of another type character.

superscript (also superior)—a small symbol, letter, or number that is positioned above and to the side of another type character.

swash—type characters with flourishes for serifs.

terminal—the end of a stroke not terminated with a serif.

text letters—typeface which resembles hand-drawn letters.

text type—type used in body copy, usually measuring from 9 to 14 points in size.

to come (TK)—an indication to the typesetter or printer that some copy is missing from the original text and will be forthcoming.

trademark—a name, symbol, or other device identifying a product that is officially registered and legally restricted to the use of the owner.

transposition (tr)—a common typographic error in which letters or words are not correctly placed.

type—generally refers to text or body type.

typeface—the surface of a body of type that makes the impression. Also the full range of type of the same design.

typesetter—the person who sets type.

type specifications (or specs)—written instructions to the typesetter or printer designating how the copy should be treated typographically.

typographic errors (or typos)—typed or typeset errors.

uppercase—capital letters.

Velox—a high-quality, copyrighted photographic paper print from which the copy is inspected before printing. The name is broadly applied in the graphic arts to any type of line or screened photoprint used for reproduction.

weight—the boldness of a typeface.

white space—any space that is not printed.

widow—the end of a paragraph or of a column of reading matter that is undesirably short.

width—the amount of horizontal space each letter covers.

word break—breaking a word on a syllable at the end of one line and continuing the word on the following line.

word spacing—spacing between individual words.

wraparound (or runaround)—erratic margins of typeset copy designed to fit around a photograph or illustration.

wrong font (wf)—a type character set in a face, style, or size other than that specified.

x—proofreader's mark used to indicate dirty or smudged copy or broken type.

x-height—the height of the main body of lowercase characters, excluding ascenders and descenders.

x-line—the line that marks the tops of lowercase characters.

INDEX